STEPHANIE CULP'S
12-Month
Organizer
and Project
Planner

D1311850

BETTERWAY BOOKS

Cincinnati, Ohio

Acknowledgments

Bill Brohaugh had the idea for this planner and provided the all-important format concepts; Mert Ransdell cemented the deal in her usual charming manner. My longtime editor, Beth Frank, lent her very talented editorial hand, and Diane Johnson was our final checkpoint at the computer. Hugh Gildea consistently completed meaningful paperwork in a timely fashion, and Boca and Fritz Culp provided their own special brand of personal input on a daily basis. Thank you all.

Edited by Beth Frank
Designed by Brian Roeth
Illustrations by Julie A. Baker

Table of Contents

If your projects include getting organized, you'll find a 12-month schedule of possible organizing projects on page 4.

Mastering the Art of Project Planning

With this planner, you can successfully plan and complete any project you care to take on. If you want to get organized, 11 months include the guidelines you'll need to streamline a particular area of your life. (August is set aside for vacation.) If getting organized is not a problem or priority for you, plan a project of your choice each month. The forms you need to plan and complete any project are found in each monthly section.

Start any time of the year and plan one project per month. (If you purchased this planner in September, for instance, begin there, and continue into the following year.) If a project is too big to finish in one month, use the next month's project forms to continue working until it's done. For getting organized, you don't have to follow the designated order of the organizing projects in the planner. For example, if you'd rather do your closets in January, flip ahead and use the May guidelines to plan your January project.

Whatever you choose to do, these Super Steps will help you get through any organizing project:

FIVE SUPER STEPS TO GETTING ORGANIZED

1. **Gather** everything in one area.
2. **Sort and group** everything, putting

PROJECT MASTER PLAN— STEPS TO SUCCESS

- Identify the problem or need.
- Recognize the solution, and set your project goal.
- Acknowledge the benefits of accomplishing that goal.
- Visualize those benefits, and write an affirmation for success.
- Realistically estimate the time you'll need to complete the project, and set a deadline for completion.
- Develop a detailed To Do list, and delegate as many tasks as possible.
- Determine what products, services or information you'll need for the project, and contact sources to price those services or products.
- Draw up a budget (if necessary) and purchase what you need and can afford.
- Schedule time on your calendar to work on the project.
- Develop a Master Plan with specific Steps to Success.
- Eliminate outdated, useless or unnecessary items and tasks.
- List your project priorities so you can tackle the most important tasks first.
- Stick to the project schedule and deadline.
- Reward yourself when you've successfully completed the project.

like items together.

3. **Eliminate** items you don't use, need or want.

4. **Organize** items logically, assigning each item a space that's as close as possible to where it's actually used. Then put everything in its place.

5. **Use organizing systems and space savers** to maximize the storage potential of your space.

To get as much as possible done in the time allotted, utilize the following project scheduling secrets:

SECRETS FOR GETTING THINGS DONE

- Be realistic about the amount of time it takes to get things done; then add a little more time than you think you need.
- Don't procrastinate; give yourself a deadline and stick to it.
- Don't allow yourself to be interrupted by phone calls, visitors or other distractions.
- Keep things simple. Don't waste valuable time by overcomplicating what you need to do to complete the project.
- Concentrate fully on the task at hand.
- Don't waste time by stalling, waffling or making excuses, when all that's needed is a simple decision.

With this in mind, use the forms provided each month, follow the Master Plan—Steps to Success, and set aside regular times each month to see your projects through to completion.

12-MONTH PROJECT MASTER PLAN

Whether you are getting organized or tackling other projects of your choice, begin by mapping out a 12-month schedule.

MONTH	PROJECT	COMMENTS
January	Organize desk	January 10 is "National Clean Off Your Desk Day"
February	Organize files	Clean out last year's papers and set up this year's files
March	Organize tax records	Get ready for April 15 tax deadline
April	Organize and clean kitchen and bathroom	Start spring cleaning
May	Organize closets and dresser drawers	Change seasonal clothes and review fashion image
June	Organize garage, attic and basement	Best weather conditions for tackling these areas
July	Sort through and catch up on reading materials	Whittle down stacks of magazines and spend some lazy days reading
August	Vacation month!	Time off is good for the spirit!
September	Organize the children's rooms	Weed out outgrown clothing and toys
October	Conquer small pockets of clutter	October is "National Get Organized Month"
November	Get organized for the holidays	Thanksgiving, Hanukkah and Christmas are just ahead
December	Organize schedule for parties and other holiday events	Give and go to parties, finish holiday preparations and enjoy the season

12-MONTH PROJECT MASTER PLAN

Use this form to plan your projects for the coming year. Follow the suggestions for getting organized, or plan a project of your own.

MONTH	PROJECT	COMMENTS
January		
February		
March		
April		
May		
June		
July		
August		
September		
October		
November		
December		

SPECIAL DATES MASTER CALENDAR

Projects are important, but you also need to spend time on yourself and your relationships. Use this Special Dates Master Calendar to enter the dates of birthdays, anniversaries, graduations and other special occasions for the next 12 months. Refer to this calendar at the beginning of each month, and plan something special for those dates.

JANUARY

DATE	SPECIAL DAY	DATE	SPECIAL DAY

FEBRUARY

DATE	SPECIAL DAY	DATE	SPECIAL DAY

MARCH

DATE	SPECIAL DAY	DATE	SPECIAL DAY

APRIL

DATE	SPECIAL DAY	DATE	SPECIAL DAY

MAY

DATE	SPECIAL DAY	DATE	SPECIAL DAY

JUNE

DATE	SPECIAL DAY	DATE	SPECIAL DAY

JULY

DATE	SPECIAL DAY		DATE	SPECIAL DAY

AUGUST

DATE	SPECIAL DAY		DATE	SPECIAL DAY

SEPTEMBER

DATE	SPECIAL DAY		DATE	SPECIAL DAY

OCTOBER

DATE	SPECIAL DAY		DATE	SPECIAL DAY

NOVEMBER

DATE	SPECIAL DAY		DATE	SPECIAL DAY

DECEMBER

DATE	SPECIAL DAY		DATE	SPECIAL DAY

"The vital, successful people I have met all had one common characteristic. They had a plan."

—Marilyn Van Derbur

PROJECT PLANNING

Make sure your New Year's resolutions include setting aside time to plan for and complete projects this year. Begin by using January's project planning forms to plan and complete a project of your choice. Mark key deadlines on your calendar.

IF YOU WANT TO GET ORGANIZED:

"National Clean Off Your Desk Day" falls in January, so if your resolutions include "getting organized," January is the perfect time to *organize your desk.*

JANUARY PROJECT PRIORITIES

Week One _____

_____

_____

_____

Week Two _____

_____

_____

_____

Week Three _____

_____

_____

_____

Week Four _____

_____

_____

_____

Week Five _____

_____

_____

_____

JANUARY CALENDAR

SUNDAY	MONDAY	TUESDAY	WEDNESDAY

THURSDAY	FRIDAY	SATURDAY

SCHEDULING CHECKLIST

✔ Schedule appointments and standing obligations.

✔ Note special days such as birthdays and anniversaries.

✔ Schedule time for regular exercise.

✔ Make a date to give time and attention to someone special.

✔ Schedule a few hours each week of quiet time for yourself.

PRIORITIZING PROJECTS

Use the forms provided to plan your month's project. Each week, prioritize your project tasks and schedule them on the Project Priorities page at the front of this calendar.

PROJECT ANALYSIS: DESK ORGANIZATION

Problem: Your desk is piled high with papers, files and other clutter; you waste time every day looking for something buried in the mess.

Solution: Go through everything inside and on top of your desk, organizing and systematizing it all.

Project Goal: Organize your desk.

Benefits: More efficient and productive working conditions; less stress.

Visualization: Visualize your desk perfectly organized.

Affirmation: My desk is always organized, and so am I. I'm efficient, productive and in control. I am always prepared for new opportunities that come my way.

Estimate of Time Needed: Depends on what has accumulated on your desk. Allow at least a full day; if it will take you longer than that, schedule on your calendar the steps you need to take so you can complete your project on time.

Deadline: January 31.

TO DO

- Shop for necessary equipment, furnishings and supplies.
- Gather all papers, files and other desk clutter.
- Sort everything into categories.
- Organize everything that goes back into the desk drawers.
- Eliminate unnecessary or outdated papers and files.
- Go through each category and decide the final disposition of the paperwork.

- Delegate and distribute as much paperwork as possible.
- Set up a streamlined desktop system.

Delegate as many tasks as possible. For example, let someone else file, or have someone presort some of the loose papers by date or category.

NEEDS CHECKLIST

You may need to invest in some new furniture and supplies to create a streamlined work setting. Exactly what you'll need will be determined by how much room you have and how much paper you process on a regular basis. You may need:

Desk with at least one drawer for small supplies and, ideally, one file drawer

Two-drawer filing cabinet placed near your desk for immediate access to files used regularly

Cabinet, bookcase or shelves to hold binders, manuals, reference books and extra office supplies

Equipment platform for typewriter, computer, adding machine, etc.

Credenza, table or rolling file cart to use as a holding/sorting area for paper-intensive projects in progress

Wood or wire In/Out boxes to sort papers into categories

File folders and labels to make new files for papers, if necessary

Hanging file folders (with clear tabs) to hold the file folders in your desk, filing cabinet or cart

Metal frames to fit inside file drawers and hold the hanging files

Drawer dividers to organize papers clips

and other small supplies

Establish a budget before making your purchases. Call around to check prices and make a shopping list. Buy what you need and can afford, and then put those tools to work to complete your project.

SOURCES

- Furniture and used office furniture stores
- Office supply and stationery stores
- Discount office supply megastores
- Office supply, equipment and furniture catalogs
- Home supply stores
- Variety stores
- Lighting stores
- Closet and organization stores

For more detailed information on how to complete this project, you may want to refer to my book *Conquering the Paper Pile-Up*.

ELIMINATE: DESK CLUTTER

- Junk mail and unsolicited flyers
- Financial brochures for investments you never made
- Outdated wall calendars with no business purpose
- Pens that don't write
- Cartoons and copies of cartoons
- Outdated school schedules
- Business cards from people you don't know or care to know
- Misprinted or outdated stationery
- Old forms that have been replaced
- Greeting cards you've received over the years
- Old road maps from other states

- Notes you made to yourself eons ago
- Outdated rubber stamps
- Expired coupons
- At least half of all the children's papers you've been saving
- Recipes you'll never have time to try
- Old travel brochures
- Old sales reports that are now un-important
- Duplicate paperwork
- Invitations with past dates
- Old checkbooks from closed bank accounts (cut them up before disposing)
- Business cards from your previous job
- Articles that were clipped and copied just because you liked them
- Expired warranties and instruction books for items you no longer have
- Magazines and journals more than three months old
- Catalogs from two seasons ago
- At least half of those pink memos from people who called you and whose call you never returned

MASTER PLAN—STEPS TO SUCCESS

Remove everything from the desk drawers. Gather all the papers and files, putting everything in several stacks, bins or boxes. Group like items together. Items that can be sorted, grouped and organized include:

PERSONAL ITEMS

Put awards on the wall and place a small selection of photos on the bookshelf or credenza. This is a work space; personal touches are nice but should be kept to a minimum.

REFERENCE BOOKLETS AND MANUALS

Store on a shelf mounted above the desk. Otherwise, on a bookcase or in a credenza. Booklets, such as instructions for the phone, can be kept under the equipment for easy access.

OFFICE SUPPLIES

Store forms and stationery that you use every day on a metal stationery storage rack placed within easy reach, or store them in hanging file folders in your desk file drawer.

FILES

There are different ways to organize papers into files. *Permanent* files are files that must be kept for legal, financial, historical or reference purposes. These should be filed, alphabetically in a filing cabinet. *Project* files are relative to an ongoing project that requires a lot of paperwork (such as lawsuits, fundraising events, and major deals involving negotiations with several people). Make up files for the different categories of research as well as for notes and drafts. A rolling cart is perfect for temporary storage of these files. When the project is completed, go through the files, eliminate unnecessary notes and research, and file whatever paperwork needs to be kept in permanent files. *Action* or *Working* files are files that you need access to every day. These can be kept in your desk file drawer, in a file rack on top of your desk or credenza, or in a file rack mounted on the wall by your desk. When you no longer need those files on a daily basis, return them to the permanent files. (For more information on organizing papers into files, see February.)

LOOSE PAPERS

Gather up all loose papers and go through them, sorting them into these five categories:

To Do
To Pay
To File
To Read
Trash

Decide to decide. Now is the time to make a commitment to making decisions about your paperwork. Stop putting papers in piles "just for now" because you can't make a decision about what to do with them. Decide to read it, file it, pay it or do it.

To Do. Dump anything you don't need to do and things that are too late to do. To ensure that you don't let your To Do basket become a burial ground, start each day by going through the box and prioritizing what needs to be done.

To Pay. If the item has been paid, mark it paid, and file it. If there's a problem with the bill, move it to your To Do pile so you'll make the call or do the research necessary to solve the problem before you actually pay the bill.

To Read. Quickly scan the table of contents or cover; if there's no sound reason for reading something, or you don't have time to read it, dump it. If the material is out of date (i.e., old catalogs or flyers), dump it. More than three months' worth of issues? Pitch at least one month's worth. Cut out any articles that you must read and staple the pages. Toss or recycle the rest of the periodical and put the article into your To Read stack.

To File. Look at each piece of paper and ask yourself if you need to keep it. Toss as much as you can. Only file papers that you need to keep for historic, legal or financial reasons.

SET UP A NEW DESKTOP SYSTEM

To keep your papers organized every day, simply set up baskets or bins for the four basic categories: To Do, To Pay, To File and To Read.

To Do and **To Pay.** Use roomy wood or stacking wire baskets. Don't get colored plastic trays that, when stacked, quickly become paper traps.

To Read. Find a big bin or basket, and keep it somewhere other than the top of your desk. When the basket gets full, toss something out before you accept one more piece of paper to read.

To File. Use an oversized wire basket (such as the kind used in rolling carts) or a large bin. Put it under your desk, and mark it clearly so it won't inadvertently be mistaken for trash.

Make Time. Set aside a regular time to pay bills, do the filing, and catch up on your reading.

REWARD YOURSELF

Once you've completed your desk organization project, give yourself a reward. Go to a movie, take a day trip, or spend next Sunday curled up with a good book. Do something enjoyable; you've earned it.

PROJECT ANALYSIS

PROBLEM OR NEED
Describe a problem you want to correct, or outline something you need or want.

_____

_____

_____

_____

_____

_____

SOLUTION AND PROJECT GOAL
Write the solution to your problem or describe what you must do to get what you need or want.

_____

_____

_____

_____

BENEFITS
List the benefits that will result if you complete your project and achieve your goal.

_____

_____

_____

_____

VISUALIZATION

Describe how you see yourself and your surroundings after you have achieved your Project Goal.

_____

_____

_____

_____

_____

AFFIRMATION

Write an affirmation for success. Review it regularly and remind yourself of the ongoing benefits of your successfully completed project.

_____

_____

_____

_____

_____

ESTIMATE TOTAL TIME NEEDED FOR PROJECT

Make certain your estimate is realistic and you are willing to set that time aside.

_____

DEADLINE FOR PROJECT COMPLETION

A goal is just a dream with a deadline. Set a sensible deadline for success.

_____

TO DO

PROJECT: _____ DEADLINE: _____

THINGS TO DO | DATE SCHEDULED

DELEGATE

PROJECT: _____ DEADLINE: _____

TODAY'S DATE	TASK	DELEGATED TO	DEADLINE	DONE

NEEDS CHECKLIST

PROJECT: _____ **DEADLINE:** _____

List sources for information, services or products you need to complete your project. Note item size, quantity, color or other details. Call beforehand to check availability and price.

NEEDS	SOURCE	PHONE NUMBER	PRICE

NOTES

_____

_____

_____

_____

_____

_____

_____

_____

_____

_____

_____

_____

_____

_____

_____

MASTER PLAN—STEPS TO SUCCESS

PROJECT: _____ DEADLINE: _____

WHERE TO START

_____

_____

_____

_____

Make a detailed list of all actions needed to complete your project. Prioritize and schedule each task on a weekly basis. (Use the Project Priorities form and your monthly calendar for planning.) When each task is completed, cross it off your list.

ACTIONS TO TAKE	DATE SCHEDULED

ACTIONS TO TAKE	DATE SCHEDULED

"I've always tried to go a step past wherever people expected me to end up."

—Beverly Sills

PROJECT PLANNING

Use February's project planning forms to plan and/or complete a project of your choice. Mark key deadlines on your calendar.

IF YOU WANT TO GET ORGANIZED:

Now that all of last year's statements have arrived in the mail, this is a good month to go through your files and set them up for this year's paperwork. February is the perfect time to *organize your files.*

FEBRUARY PROJECT PRIORITIES

Week One _____

_____

_____

_____

Week Two _____

_____

_____

_____

Week Three _____

_____

_____

_____

Week Four _____

_____

_____

_____

Week Five _____

_____

_____

_____

FEBRUARY CALENDAR

SUNDAY	MONDAY	TUESDAY	WEDNESDAY

THURSDAY	FRIDAY	SATURDAY

SCHEDULING CHECKLIST

✔ Schedule appointments and standing obligations.

✔ Note special days such as birthdays and anniversaries.

✔ Schedule time for regular exercise.

✔ Make a date to give time and attention to someone special.

✔ Schedule a few hours each week of quiet time for yourself.

PRIORITIZING PROJECTS

Use the forms provided to plan your month's project. Each week, prioritize your project tasks and schedule them on the Project Priorities page at the front of this calendar.

PROJECT ANALYSIS: ORGANIZATION OF FILES

Problem: Files are stuffed to bursting with all manner of paperwork, including duplicates and irrelevant or unnecessary documents. Something filed yesterday may not be there today.

Solution: Go through all the files, purging and organizing them.

Project Goal: To organize your files.

Benefits: Less time wasted looking for misfiled papers and documents. You'll be more efficient and in control.

Visualization: Visualize your files perfectly organized.

Affirmation: My files are organized and easy to understand. I can retrieve a document or file quickly and effortlessly. What I need is at my fingertips, and I can respond immediately to anything involving paperwork.

Estimate of Time Needed: Depends on your files. Allow a minimum of four to six hours per standard-sized filing drawer. If you can't get through all the files in one sitting, put a red dot on all the files you've done so you'll know which are left. If the project takes longer than you anticipate, break it into clearly defined segments (e.g., commit to going through at least 30 files each week until you have completed the project). Then schedule time on your calendar to work on those segments.

Deadline: February 28.

TO DO

- Shop for necessary equipment and supplies.
- Evaluate current filing system, and make a list of primary file categories, if any.
- Make a preliminary list of major topics/subjects that should have a file.
- Go through each file folder—one at a time—and decide what to do with those papers and that file.
- Purge duplicate and other unnecessary files and papers.
- Store important archival files in banker's boxes in another area.
- Make sure each manila folder has a hanging folder with a clearly written or typed label to match the label on the manila folder.
- Refile misfiled papers, and consolidate duplicate files.
- Make new files where necessary. Make the labels concise and easy to read.
- Organize the drawers, making final changes if necessary. Label each drawer.

Delegate as many tasks as possible. For example, have someone check for and eliminate duplicate files. Or have them put papers in the files in chronological order, making it easier for you to go through the file and make decisions about its contents.

NEEDS CHECKLIST

Although you're purging your files, you still may need extra storage. The exact number of items you'll need will be determined by how many files you have to organize. You may need:

File folders and labels to make new files

Hanging file folders to hold files. If your filing cabinet drawers weren't designed to hold hanging files, purchase an inexpensive frame insert for each drawer.

Clear tabs for hanging file folders in case you need to relabel existing hanging file folders

Banker's boxes to store important archival records

Establish a budget before making your purchases. Call around to check prices and make a shopping list. Buy what you need and can afford, and then put those tools to work to complete your project.

SOURCES

- Furniture and used office furniture stores
- Office supply and stationery stores
- Discount office supply megastores
- Office supply, equipment and furniture catalogs

For more detailed information on how to complete this project, you may want to refer to my book *Conquering the Paper Pile-Up*.

ELIMINATE: FILES AND PAPERS

- Files for projects that never got off the ground
- Financial brochures for investments you never made
- Old sales reports that are now irrelevant
- Duplicate paperwork
- Meaningless cover letters
- Mindless correspondence
- Brochures and flyers from vendors that you never use
- Outdated schedules
- Outdated price lists
- Forms that have been replaced with a new version
- Articles that you clipped and copied just because you liked them
- Cartoons and copies of cartoons
- Invitations with dates that have passed
- Paid bill receipts that were never tax deductible (such as department store receipts from three years ago)
- Old travel brochures
- Expired warranties and instruction books for items you no longer have
- Policies that have expired and been replaced with other policies
- Recipes you'll never have time to try
- At least half of all the children's papers you've been saving
- Outdated resource and reference materials (such as that paper you wrote in college 15 years ago)

MASTER PLAN— STEPS TO SUCCESS

An alphabetical filing system is the easiest to use. Within that system, you may want to break some files out into specific categories, such as:

- Business
- Legal
- Clients
- Personal
- Financial
- Real Estate
- General
- Reference/resource

After listing your categories, determine which subject headings will fall under each. Here are some possible ways to label files with category headings first, followed by the subject headings:

BUSINESS

- Accounts payable
- Accounts receivable
- Correspondence

- Expenses
- General information
- Suppliers/vendors

CLIENTS
- List alphabetically by client or company name

FINANCIAL
- Auto:
  Gasoline
  Payments
  Registration
  Repairs

- House:
  Improvements
  Inventory
  Mortgage
  Repairs

- Receipts:
  American
    Express
  Department
    stores
  MasterCard
  Miscellaneous
  Office supplies
  Petty cash
  Postage
  Visa

- Insurance:
  Auto
  Health
  House
  Life

- Investments:
  Pension plan
  Savings
  Stocks and bonds

- Taxes:
  Information
  Returns (note year)
  Return backup information (note year)

- Utilities:
  Electric
  Gas and oil
  Sewer
  Telephone

GENERAL
- Children's records (subdivide by child)
- Correspondence
- Health information and medical records
- Pet records

- Product information
- Warranties and instructions

LEGAL
- File alphabetically (by case name). Keep all records in strict chronological order. Separate expenses. For example:

  Culp vs. Reed
  Culp vs. Reed—Expenses

For major cases, divide records into several files according to the nature of the documents.

PERSONAL
- Birth certificate
- Career information
- Correspondence
- Family history
- Resumes
- Will

REAL ESTATE
- File alphabetically by property location if there are several properties.
  For example:

  Miami Condo
  3824 Ocean Avenue

  New York Apartment
  208 W. 23rd Street

  Prescott Cabin

REFERENCE/RESOURCE
- Art
- Articles

- Children's camps
- Day trips
- Decorating ideas
- Family history
- Repair services
- Restaurants
- Travel
- Vendors

Next, go through your existing files, one at a time. Do one of three things with each paper in the file:

Purge the paper or file by throwing it away.

Store the paper or file in a banker's box. Clearly mark each folder and the front of the box with the contents and the date. Store the box elsewhere—in a records storage facility, a cabinet or closet. Periodically purge these storage boxes by date. For example, you can safely toss a box of 10-year-old receipts.

File the paper or file chronologically in the proper file. Make a new file if necessary. Toss duplicate paperwork; consolidate duplicate files. For example, you might find a file marked *Insurance—Health* (filed under *I*), and a file marked *Health Insurance* (filed under *H*), thus scattering and duplicating your records into two separate files. Eliminate duplication by combining the paperwork into one file.

NEW FILES

You may need to make some new files. The new files will be for categories you incorporate, or to hold papers that you never filed in the first place (because no file existed).

Name the file so it's logical for you. If you need a file for Andrews Plumbing, but you're more likely to think of "Plumbing" than "Andrews," label the file *Plumbing—Andrews*.

Check to be sure that everything is filed in alphabetical order. Make any necessary changes (such as revising a file name that doesn't fit within your system), and mark the outside of the drawer to indicate what categories of files are inside.

REWARD YOURSELF

Once you've finished your file organization project, give yourself a reward. Go out to dinner or to a concert, go away for the weekend, or get a group of friends together for an afternoon or evening of hilarity. Celebrate—you've earned it.

PROJECT ANALYSIS

PROBLEM OR NEED

Describe a problem you want to correct, or outline something you need or want.

_____

_____

_____

_____

_____

_____

SOLUTION AND PROJECT GOAL

Write the solution to your problem or describe what you must do to get what you need or want.

_____

_____

_____

_____

BENEFITS

List the benefits that will result if you complete your project and achieve your goal.

_____

_____

_____

_____

VISUALIZATION

Describe how you see yourself and your surroundings after you have achieved your Project Goal.

_____

_____

_____

_____

_____

AFFIRMATION

Write an affirmation for success. Review it regularly and remind yourself of the ongoing benefits of your successfully completed project.

_____

_____

_____

_____

_____

ESTIMATE TOTAL TIME NEEDED FOR PROJECT

Make certain your estimate is realistic and you are willing to set that time aside.

_____

DEADLINE FOR PROJECT COMPLETION

A goal is just a dream with a deadline. Set a sensible deadline for success.

_____

TO DO

PROJECT: _____ DEADLINE: _____

THINGS TO DO	DATE SCHEDULED

DELEGATE

PROJECT: _____ **DEADLINE:** _____

TODAY'S DATE	TASK	DELEGATED TO	DEADLINE	DONE

NEEDS CHECKLIST

PROJECT: _____ **DEADLINE:** _____

List sources for information, services or products you need to complete your project. Note item size, quantity, color or other details. Call beforehand to check availability and price.

NEEDS	SOURCE	PHONE NUMBER	PRICE

NOTES

_____

_____

_____

_____

_____

_____

_____

_____

_____

_____

_____

_____

_____

_____

_____

MASTER PLAN—STEPS TO SUCCESS

PROJECT: _____ DEADLINE: _____

WHERE TO START

_____

_____

_____

_____

_____

Make a detailed list of all actions needed to complete your project. Prioritize and schedule each task on a weekly basis. (Use the Project Priorities form and your monthly calendar for planning.) When each task is completed, cross it off your list.

ACTIONS TO TAKE	DATE SCHEDULED

ACTIONS TO TAKE | DATE SCHEDULED

"The difference between the impossible and the possible lies in a man's determination."

—Tommy Lasorda

PROJECT PLANNING

Use March's project planning forms to plan and/or complete a project of your choice. Mark key deadlines on your calendar.

IF YOU WANT TO GET ORGANIZED:

Rather than wait until the last minute in April, March is the perfect time to organize last year's financial records in preparation for filing your tax return on, or before, April 15. Use March to *organize your tax records and receipts.*

MARCH PROJECT PRIORITIES

Week One _____

_____

_____

_____

Week Two _____

_____

_____

_____

Week Three _____

_____

_____

_____

Week Four _____

_____

_____

_____

Week Five _____

_____

_____

_____

MARCH CALENDAR

SUNDAY	MONDAY	TUESDAY	WEDNESDAY

THURSDAY	FRIDAY	SATURDAY

SCHEDULING CHECKLIST

✔ Schedule appointments and standing obligations.

✔ Note special days such as birthdays and anniversaries.

✔ Schedule time for regular exercise.

✔ Make a date to give time and attention to someone special.

✔ Schedule a few hours each week of quiet time for yourself.

PRIORITIZING PROJECTS

Use the forms provided to plan your month's project. Each week, prioritize your project tasks and schedule them on the Project Priorities page at the front of this calendar.

PROJECT ANALYSIS: TAX RECORDS AND RECEIPTS

Problem: April 15 will soon be here; you must organize your financial records and receipts before you can file your tax return.

Solution: Gather all financial and tax-related records and receipts and organize them well in advance of the filing deadline.

Project Goal: To organize your tax records and receipts.

Benefits: Eliminate the stress and anxiety caused by waiting until the last minute to complete your tax return. By setting up a simple system to keep tax-related records organized as they come in, this won't be a major project next year.

Visualization: Visualize your financial records in perfect order, with your tax return completed well in advance of the deadline.

Affirmation: My financial records and receipts are always organized. At any time during the year, it's easy to locate any and all financial paperwork—for whatever reason. Gathering information for my yearly tax return can be done easily and quickly, well in advance of the tax deadline.

Estimate of Time Needed: Depends on how disorganized your records and receipts are, and how complicated your tax situation is. Begin by scheduling one full day. If you don't finish, schedule more time later in the month.

Deadline: March 31. (You could make it April 15, but then you'd be doing it at the last minute, which is stressful and unnecessary.)

TO DO

- Shop for necessary equipment and supplies.
- Gather all tax-related records and receipts from drawers, stacks, boxes and existing files.
- Sort the records and receipts, and put them in manila envelopes labeled by category and year.
- Use the front of each envelope to recap the amounts inside.
- Total each envelope.
- Use the envelope totals to formulate how you complete your tax return, or give the envelopes to your accountant if he or she needs the information to complete your return.
- Once the return is filed, store the envelopes in a banker's box labeled with the contents and year.

Delegate as many tasks as possible. For example, have someone group your receipts by category or presort them by date.

NEEDS CHECKLIST

You'll need supplies to sort this year's records and store future financial records and receipts. (For information on the supplies you need and how to set up the files, see February's project, "Organize Your Files.") For now you may need:

Manila clasp envelopes (9″ × 12″ or 10″ × 13″) to categorize and store statements and receipts

Banker's boxes to store the records and receipts when you're done with them

Plastic boxes (shoe or sweater size) to

store bank statements and canceled checks

Before you buy anything, call around to check prices. Make a shopping list. Purchase what you need, then put those tools to work for you to complete your project.

SOURCES

- Office supply and stationery stores
- Discount office supply megastores
- Office supply catalogs
- Variety stores

For more detailed information, you can refer to my book *Conquering the Paper Pile-Up*.

ELIMINATE: NONDEDUCTIBLE RECEIPTS

Toss any nondeductible receipts that have no other significance (such as legal or budget-related).

MASTER PLAN— STEPS TO SUCCESS

Gather all records and receipts in one large box. The box should have a lid so you don't accidentally toss in unrelated papers.

Go through the box(es) and sort everything into manila envelopes that are clearly labeled by category and year. For example:

- American Express (year)
- Office Supplies (year)

(For a list of common financial categories, see February's project, "Organize Your Files.")

Your tax-deductible categories depend on your particular circumstances. Call your accountant or tax preparer for more specific guidelines regarding tax deductions.

Once you've sorted everything into the envelopes, recap the figures. For example:

Petty Cash (Year)

Office Supplies	$1,502.45
Travel—Taxis	352.90
Client Gifts	175.00
Total:	$2,030.35

Use the envelope totals to compile your tax return, or give the information to your tax preparer. Copy the recap information onto a few sheets of paper, keeping one copy for yourself and giving one copy to your tax preparer.

Store Your Financial Records and Receipts. Make a copy of your completed tax returns for your records. Store the labeled envelopes in a banker's box labeled *Financial Records (year)*. Put your tax return in the box, or keep it with your active files if you think you might need to refer to it in the coming year. Store the banker's box elsewhere, keeping only those financial records for the current year in your active filing system.

REWARD YOURSELF

Once you've organized your tax records and receipts—without waiting until the last possible minute—give yourself a reward. If you're due for a refund, plan to either spend it on something delightful, or invest it for your future. If you owe taxes, your reward will perhaps be a bit more subdued. Go hiking, spend a weekend in bed with good books, or take in three movies in a row. Whatever you do, relax; the stress of getting your return done is now behind you.

PROJECT ANALYSIS

PROBLEM OR NEED

Describe a problem you want to correct, or outline something you need or want.

_____

_____

_____

_____

_____

_____

SOLUTION AND PROJECT GOAL

Write the solution to your problem or describe what you must do to get what you need or want.

_____

_____

_____

_____

BENEFITS

List the benefits that will result if you complete your project and achieve your goal.

_____

_____

_____

_____

VISUALIZATION

Describe how you see yourself and your surroundings after you have achieved your Project Goal.

_____

_____

_____

_____

_____

AFFIRMATION

Write an affirmation for success. Review it regularly and remind yourself of the ongoing benefits of your successfully completed project.

_____

_____

_____

_____

_____

ESTIMATE TOTAL TIME NEEDED FOR PROJECT

Make certain your estimate is realistic and you are willing to set that time aside.

_____

DEADLINE FOR PROJECT COMPLETION

A goal is just a dream with a deadline. Set a sensible deadline for success.

_____

TO DO

PROJECT: _____ DEADLINE: _____

THINGS TO DO	DATE SCHEDULED

DELEGATE

PROJECT: _____ **DEADLINE:** _____

TODAY'S DATE	TASK	DELEGATED TO	DEADLINE	DONE

NEEDS CHECKLIST

PROJECT: _____ **DEADLINE:** _____

List sources for information, services or products you need to complete your project. Note item size, quantity, color or other details. Call beforehand to check availability and price.

NEEDS	SOURCE	PHONE NUMBER	PRICE

NOTES

MASTER PLAN—STEPS TO SUCCESS

PROJECT: _____ DEADLINE: _____

WHERE TO START

_____

_____

_____

_____

_____

Make a detailed list of all actions needed to complete your project. Prioritize and schedule each task on a weekly basis. (Use the Project Priorities form and your monthly calendar for planning.) When each task is completed, cross it off your list.

ACTIONS TO TAKE	DATE SCHEDULED

ACTIONS TO TAKE	DATE SCHEDULED

"Find something you're passionate about and keep tremendously interested in it."

—Julia Child

PROJECT PLANNING

Use April's project planning forms to plan and/or complete a project of your choice. Mark key deadlines on your calendar.

IF YOU WANT TO GET ORGANIZED:

Spring is traditionally a time of transition and brings with it the opportunity to open the windows and do some spring cleaning. A thorough cleaning is always more effective when things are organized. April is the perfect time to *organize kitchen and bathroom cupboards and drawers.*

APRIL PROJECT PRIORITIES

Week One _____

_____

_____

_____

Week Two _____

_____

_____

_____

Week Three _____

_____

_____

_____

Week Four _____

_____

_____

_____

Week Five _____

_____

_____

_____

APRIL CALENDAR

SUNDAY	MONDAY	TUESDAY	WEDNESDAY

THURSDAY	FRIDAY	SATURDAY

SCHEDULING CHECKLIST

✔ Schedule appointments and standing obligations.

✔ Note special days such as birthdays and anniversaries.

✔ Schedule time for regular exercise.

✔ Make a date to give time and attention to someone special.

✔ Schedule a few hours each week of quiet time for yourself.

PRIORITIZING PROJECTS

Use the forms provided to plan your month's project. Each week, prioritize your project tasks and schedule them on the Project Priorities page at the front of this calendar.

PROJECT ANALYSIS: KITCHEN AND BATHROOM ORGANIZATION

Problem: Cupboards are crammed with clutter, and drawers are overflowing. You can't find items when you need them, and some things are likely to fall over or spill if you try to retrieve an item quickly.

Solution: Go through cabinets and drawers in the kitchen and bathroom, organizing what you need and use on a regular basis.

Project Goal: To organize your kitchen and bathroom cupboards and drawers.

Benefits: Items will be easy to find and put away, and cupboards and drawers will be easier to keep clean.

Visualization: Visualize all of your kitchen and bathroom cupboards and drawers perfectly organized.

Affirmation: The cupboards and drawers in my kitchen and bathroom are always clean and organized. Cooking and grooming are free of the frustration that goes along with cluttered cabinets and drawers. Keeping those areas clean is a simple matter that requires minimal time and attention.

Estimate of Time Needed: Depends on how many cupboards and drawers you have to organize. Allow at least one full day to tackle the project. If you don't finish, schedule the steps you still need to do on the calendar to complete your project.

Deadline: April 30

TO DO

- Measure the inside of your cupboards and drawers.
- Taking the measurements with you, shop for organizing and space-saving gadgets that will fit the inside spaces.
- Working on one area at a time, take everything out of the cupboard or drawer.
- Sort items into categories.
- Eliminate items you no longer use or that are unnecessary duplicates.
- Clean the empty shelves and drawers.
- Install the organizers and space savers.
- Put everything back in, keeping like items together. Place those items as close to their logical point of use as possible.
- Take unwanted items that are in good condition to a charitable organization.

Delegate as many tasks as possible. For example, have someone clean the cupboards when you empty them, and let someone else take the unwanted items to a charity.

NEEDS CHECKLIST

You may want some space-expanding organizers for your cupboards and drawers. Exactly what you need will be determined by the inside dimensions and what you keep in that space. You may need:

Shelving, which can be added to cupboards without enough shelf space. This is also good to hang on the wall to hold items like spices in the kitchen and towels in the bathroom.

Turntables to hold small bottles and cans (like spices)

Pull-out racks for lower cabinets where cleaning supplies or canned goods are stored

Drawer dividers to help keep items organized within drawers

Hooks to free up cupboard space by

allowing you to hang things on the wall or door. These work well for items like pots and pans in the kitchen and hair ribbons or robes in the bathroom.

Over-the-door racks to extend storage possibilities. Use on the inside of the pantry door or on the back of the bathroom door to hold shampoos, sprays and lotions.

Baskets, bins or plastic containers to hold specific categories of smaller items, such as manicure tools and nail polishes

Establish a budget before you make your purchases. Call around to check prices and make a shopping list. Buy what you need and can afford, and then put those tools to work for you to complete your project.

SOURCES

- Variety stores and home supply stores
- Closet and bath organization stores
- Hardware stores

For more detailed information on how to complete this project, you may want to refer to my book *How to Conquer Clutter*.

ELIMINATE: KITCHEN CLUTTER

Rarely or Never Used

- Electric popcorn popper, skillet and knife sharpener
- Broken appliances and parts that don't go to anything
- Exotic spices
- Gourmet gadgets and doodads
- Overcomplicated food processor or blender
- Cloth napkins and corny placemats

- Joke aprons and burned potholders
- Bakeware—angel food cake tin, muffin tins
- 15-year-old pressure cooker
- Fondue pot and warming trays
- Sets of special-occasion china and glassware
- Elaborate serving dishes and utensils

Duplicates

- Can and bottle openers
- Measuring cups and spoon sets
- Peelers and parers
- Tea strainers and coffee scoops

Too Abundant

- Spatulas and wooden cooking utensils
- Empty margarine tubs, food storage containers, mayonnaise and jelly jars
- Lids that don't go with anything
- Teapots, coffee mugs and drinking glasses
- Extra sets of dishes
- Recipes and cookbooks
- Paper bags

ELIMINATE: BATHROOM CLUTTER

- Expired prescriptions and over-the-counter medicines
- Out-of-fashion makeup or makeup over one year old (old makeup is a breeding ground for bacteria)
- Stretched-out braces and bandage wraps

- Hair accessories, blow dryers, curling irons or rollers that you stopped using when you cut your hair
- Anything that has dried up, ossified, or reached a meltdown state
- Old toothbrushes
- Clogged tubes of toothpaste and ointments
- Hair sprays, perfumes, or other aerosol items that have jammed
- Bedpans or other hospital-like equipment that's no longer needed and only brings up bad memories

MASTER PLAN— STEPS TO SUCCESS

Start in either the kitchen or the bathroom and work in that room until it's finished. Begin with one area, such as the cupboards that hold the pots and pans or the drawers that hold large cooking utensils. Take everything out of the cupboard(s) or drawer(s). Group everything into categories, such as:

KITCHEN

Pots and pans
Skillets
Baking and roasting pans
Special appliances (such as electric knife sharpener)
Cooking utensils and wooden spoons
Miscellaneous utensils (such as can opener)
Sharp knives
Trash bags, food storage bags
Cleaning supplies
Dish towels, aprons, potholders
Placemats and napkins

Everyday dishes
Coffee mugs
Glasses
Spices
Coffee, teas, sweeteners
Oils, vinegars, condiments
Cereals
Boxed goods (such as pancake mix)
Canned goods
Baking ingredients
Rice, beans, pasta
Potatoes and onions
Pet food
Serving dishes
Special-occasion dishes
Wine glasses and good crystal
Good silver flatware
Serving utensils
Everyday flatware

BATHROOM

Shampoo and hair rinses
Brushes and combs
Blow dryer, curling iron
Hair accessories
Styling gels and hair sprays
Razors and shaving lotions
Bath oils and bubble bath
Lipsticks
Hand lotion and moisturizing cream
Eye makeup
Base makeup and blushes
Toothpaste and dental floss
Toothbrushes
Prescription medicines
Antacids, aspirin, cold tablets and sprays
Bandages and antiseptic ointments
Sunscreen lotions

Nail polishes, remover and manicure tools
Extra towels and washcloths
Extra toilet paper and soap
Cleaning supplies

Clean and Organize. Clean the shelves and the inside of the drawers, and put items back, organized by category. Use extra shelves, space savers and organizers. Put away items as close to their point of use as possible. Store things you use only occasionally in harder-to-reach areas, such as cabinet space above your head. Make sure medicines and cleaning supplies are stored in locked areas or safely out of reach of children and pets.

Counter Tops. Organize your counter tops by category. Eliminate what you don't need or rarely use. Keep on the counters only what is necessary, and place those items close to where they're used.

Recipes and Cookbooks. If you have an abundance of recipes and cookbooks, weed them out by tossing the clippings and giving some of the books away. Put the remaining cookbooks on a wall-mounted shelf. Store the clipped and handwritten recipes in one or two large binders, organized by category.

Paper Clutter. If there is an area in the kitchen that's a drop-off spot for mail and other papers, organize those papers according to the suggestions in January, February and March of this project planner.

REWARD YOURSELF

Once you've completed your cupboard and drawer project, give yourself a reward. Pamper yourself with a facial and a lingering bubble bath in your newly organized bathroom. Or prepare a special meal or bake your favorite cake to celebrate not only your organizational accomplishment, but also the arrival of spring.

PROJECT ANALYSIS

PROBLEM OR NEED
Describe a problem you want to correct, or outline something you need or want.

_____

_____

_____

_____

_____

_____

SOLUTION AND PROJECT GOAL
Write the solution to your problem or describe what you must do to get what you need or want.

_____

_____

_____

_____

BENEFITS
List the benefits that will result if you complete your project and achieve your goal.

_____

_____

_____

_____

VISUALIZATION

Describe how you see yourself and your surroundings after you have achieved your Project Goal.

_____

_____

_____

_____

_____

AFFIRMATION

Write an affirmation for success. Review it regularly and remind yourself of the ongoing benefits of your successfully completed project.

_____

_____

_____

_____

_____

ESTIMATE TOTAL TIME NEEDED FOR PROJECT

Make certain your estimate is realistic and you are willing to set that time aside.

_____

DEADLINE FOR PROJECT COMPLETION

A goal is just a dream with a deadline. Set a sensible deadline for success.

_____

TO DO

PROJECT: _____ **DEADLINE:** _____

THINGS TO DO	DATE SCHEDULED

DELEGATE

PROJECT: _____ **DEADLINE:** _____

TODAY'S DATE	TASK	DELEGATED TO	DEADLINE	DONE

NEEDS CHECKLIST

PROJECT: _____ **DEADLINE:** _____

List sources for information, services or products you need to complete your project. Note item size, quantity, color or other details. Call beforehand to check availability and price.

NEEDS	SOURCE	PHONE NUMBER	PRICE

NOTES

MASTER PLAN—STEPS TO SUCCESS

PROJECT: _____ DEADLINE: _____

WHERE TO START

_____

_____

_____

_____

_____

Make a detailed list of all actions needed to complete your project. Prioritize and schedule each task on a weekly basis. (Use the Project Priorities form and your monthly calendar for planning.) When each task is completed, cross it off your list.

ACTIONS TO TAKE	DATE SCHEDULED

ACTIONS TO TAKE	DATE SCHEDULED

"The greatest thing in this world is not so much where we are, but in what direction we are moving."

—Oliver Wendell Holmes

PROJECT PLANNING

Use May's project planning forms to plan and/or complete a project of your choice. Mark key deadlines on your calendar.

IF YOU WANT TO GET ORGANIZED:

May opens the door to summer, and with the warm weather comes a seasonal change of clothing. Even in climates that are warm year round, May is usually just the right time to *organize closets and dresser drawers.*

MAY PROJECT PRIORITIES

Week One _____

_____

_____

_____

Week Two _____

_____

_____

_____

Week Three _____

_____

_____

_____

Week Four _____

_____

_____

_____

Week Five _____

_____

_____

_____

MAY CALENDAR

SUNDAY	MONDAY	TUESDAY	WEDNESDAY

THURSDAY	FRIDAY	SATURDAY

SCHEDULING CHECKLIST

✔ Schedule appointments and standing obligations.

✔ Note special days such as birthdays and anniversaries.

✔ Schedule time for regular exercise.

✔ Make a date to give time and attention to someone special.

✔ Schedule a few hours each week of quiet time for yourself.

PRIORITIZING PROJECTS

Use the forms provided to plan your month's project. Each week, prioritize your project tasks and schedule them on the Project Priorities page at the front of this calendar.

PROJECT ANALYSIS: CLOSET AND DRAWER ORGANIZATION

Problem: Closets and drawers are haphazardly stuffed with all manner of things, including clothes you never wear. Clothes are often too wrinkled to wear when you pull them out, and coordinating outfits is almost impossible.

Solution: Go through all of your closets and dresser drawers, and weed out what you don't need or wear. Organize what you do wear.

Project Goal: To organize your closets and dresser drawers.

Benefits: When you pull a garment out of the closet or a drawer, it won't be crushed and wrinkled. It will be easy to dress quickly and fashionably, since your closets and drawers will be organized with only coordinating clothes that fit.

Visualization: Visualize all of your closets and dresser drawers perfectly organized.

Affirmation: All of my closets and dresser drawers are beautifully organized, making it easy to dress quickly and attractively every day. This means that I won't be late for appointments or events, and that I'll always put my best foot forward by dressing with polish and ease for both my professional and my personal life.

Estimate of Time Needed: Depends on the size and number of closets and drawers you must organize. Allow at least one full day to tackle the project. If it takes more than one uninterrupted day, schedule the steps you need to take on your calendar.

Deadline: May 31

TO DO

- Measure the inside of your closet shelves and drawers.
- Taking the measurements with you, shop for organizing and space-saving gadgets, shelf extenders and hooks that will fit inside your closets and drawers.
- Working on one closet or dresser at a time, take everything out.
- Sort items into categories.
- Eliminate items that are no longer or rarely worn.
- Install the organizers, shelf extenders and hooks.
- Put everything back into the closet or drawers, keeping like items grouped together. Where appropriate, separate the categories according to seasonal use, casual vs. dressy use, etc.
- Take unwanted items that are in good condition to a charitable organization.

Delegate as many tasks as possible. For example, find someone to install new rods, shelves and hooks. Get someone to take your unwanted items to a charity.

NEEDS CHECKLIST

You may want to invest in some space-savers and organizers for your closets and dresser drawers. Your exact needs will be determined by the quantity of items you have and the amount of closet and dresser space you have to store those items. You may need:

Shelving and shelf extenders to hang over the toilet for bathroom linens or to add to closet shelving. These allow the shelves to accommodate more items and eliminates toppling piles of clothes.

Hooks and racks. Use a shoe rack, tie rack or belt rack to group and hold those items. Hooks on doors can hold robes, nightwear and special garments, or they can add extra hanging space.

Extra rod to double closet space for everything except dresses

Drawer dividers and plastic shoeboxes to keep underwear, socks and smaller items neatly organized and to add more overall storage to the drawers

Special plastic hangers with a wire swivel hook to make it easier to hang clothing, and add-on skirt hangers to help increase the amount of hanging space available on the closet rod

Small plastic bags to separate and store stockings or other small items

Establish a budget before you make your purchases. Call around to check prices and make a shopping list. Buy what you need and can afford, and then put those tools to work for you to complete your project.

SOURCES

- Home supply and variety stores
- Closet and bath organization stores

For more detailed information on how to complete this project, you may want to refer to my book *How to Conquer Clutter*.

ELIMINATE: CLOTHING, ACCESSORIES AND LINENS

- Wire or plastic hangers from the dry cleaner
- Clothes that are hopelessly out of date
- Clothes that have become two or three sizes too small
- Shoes that hurt your feet
- Handbags that are dated or worn
- Hats that are crushed beyond resurrection
- Exhausted lingerie
- Dressy clothes and gowns you haven't worn in years
- Clothes with stains that cannot be removed
- Clothes that have needed mending for years
- Clothes that don't match the quality of what you currently wear
- Coats that are too short or too tight to wear comfortably over your regular clothes
- Stockings with runs and socks with holes
- Some of your oversupply of funky weekend "work" clothes
- Sweaters with noticeable snags or fuzz balls
- Separates you never wear because they don't go with anything
- Clothes that are too revealing for your current age, body shape and lifestyle
- Clothes that you keep for sentimental reasons only. (Keep your baptismal dress, bridal dress and letter sweater in a tissue-lined box, but get rid of the platform shoes from the 1970s.)
- Scarves you never use
- Costume jewelry that is broken or never worn
- Sneakers that are too foul to wear anymore
- Linens that are so shabby they should be turned into rags

MASTER PLAN— STEPS TO SUCCESS

Start with your main closet or one dresser, and work on it until it's completely organized.

Take everything out. Group items into categories. Common categories include:

Shirts and blouses

Skirts

Slacks

Suits

Jackets

Ties

Dressy clothes and gowns

Sweaters

Robes

Pajamas

Underwear

Coats

Belts

Scarves

Shoes

Hats

Purses

Shoe-polish equipment

Exercise clothes

Shorts

T-shirts

Socks

Travel bags

Gloves

Refold items that belong on shelves and in drawers before you put them back, and rehang clothes on plastic hangers (with swivel hooks). Group items by category, or divide the clothes according to use:

• Casual and play clothes together

• Professional or work clothes together

• Dressy and evening clothes together

You can also organize the closets by seasonal clothing: winter clothes in one area, coats in another area, summer clothes somewhere else.

Add shelving wherever possible to free dresser drawer space. Items that can be folded and stored on easy-to-reach closet shelves include:

Sweaters

Hats

Purses

Travel bags

T-shirts

Winter scarves

Sweatsuits

Keep items you use only occasionally in harder-to-access areas, such as on high shelves in the closet.

Use drawer dividers to keep items organized. Items that can be sorted and separated in drawers include:

Socks and stockings

Jewelry

Exercise tights and tops

Scarves and gloves

To organize the linen closet, eliminate linens that are no longer useful. If you have several beds of different sizes you might be able to organize the linens according to their size: all twin linens can be grouped together on one shelf, all double linens on another shelf, and all queen/king linens on a third shelf. Or you can put bed linens on a closet shelf in the bedroom they belong to.

Organize your table linens by color and category, with the special-occasion table linens stored together and everyday table linens stored together.

Bathroom towels can be organized by color so that the towel and washcloth sets are easy to see and pull out.

Organize the hall closet just as you would any other closet.

REWARD YOURSELF

Once you've organized your closets, reward yourself with a bit of shopping to update or complete your newly streamlined wardrobe. Treat yourself to a lovely lunch while you're at it.

PROJECT ANALYSIS

PROBLEM OR NEED

Describe a problem you want to correct, or outline something you need or want.

_____

_____

_____

_____

_____

_____

SOLUTION AND PROJECT GOAL

Write the solution to your problem or describe what you must do to get what you need or want.

_____

_____

_____

_____

BENEFITS

List the benefits that will result if you complete your project and achieve your goal.

_____

_____

_____

_____

VISUALIZATION

Describe how you see yourself and your surroundings after you have achieved your Project Goal.

_____

_____

_____

_____

_____

AFFIRMATION

Write an affirmation for success. Review it regularly and remind yourself of the ongoing benefits of your successfully completed project.

_____

_____

_____

_____

_____

ESTIMATE TOTAL TIME NEEDED FOR PROJECT

Make certain your estimate is realistic and you are willing to set that time aside.

_____

DEADLINE FOR PROJECT COMPLETION

A goal is just a dream with a deadline. Set a sensible deadline for success.

_____

TO DO

PROJECT: _____ **DEADLINE:** _____

THINGS TO DO   DATE SCHEDULED

DELEGATE

PROJECT: _____ **DEADLINE:** _____

TODAY'S DATE	TASK	DELEGATED TO	DEADLINE	DONE

NEEDS CHECKLIST

PROJECT: _____ **DEADLINE:** _____

List sources for information, services or products you need to complete your project. Note item size, quantity, color or other details. Call beforehand to check availability and price.

NEEDS	SOURCE	PHONE NUMBER	PRICE

NOTES

MASTER PLAN—STEPS TO SUCCESS

PROJECT: _____ **DEADLINE:** _____

WHERE TO START

_____

_____

_____

_____

_____

Make a detailed list of all actions needed to complete your project. Prioritize and schedule each task on a weekly basis. (Use the Project Priorities form and your monthly calendar for planning.) When each task is completed, cross it off your list.

ACTIONS TO TAKE	DATE SCHEDULED

ACTIONS TO TAKE	DATE SCHEDULED

"Doing the best at this moment puts you in the best place for the next moment."

—Oprah Winfrey

PROJECT PLANNING

Use June's project planning forms to plan and/or complete a project of your choice. Mark key deadlines on your calendar.

IF YOU WANT TO GET ORGANIZED:

In many parts of the country, June offers perfect weather for working outside. It's neither too hot nor too cold. With that in mind, June is the best time to *clean out and organize the garage, attic and/or basement.*

JUNE PROJECT PRIORITIES

Week One _____

_____

_____

_____

Week Two _____

_____

_____

_____

Week Three _____

_____

_____

_____

Week Four _____

_____

_____

_____

Week Five _____

_____

_____

_____

JUNE CALENDAR

SUNDAY	MONDAY	TUESDAY	WEDNESDAY

THURSDAY	FRIDAY	SATURDAY

SCHEDULING CHECKLIST

✔ Schedule appointments and standing obligations.

✔ Note special days such as birthdays and anniversaries.

✔ Schedule time for regular exercise.

✔ Make a date to give time and attention to someone special.

✔ Schedule a few hours each week of quiet time for yourself.

PRIORITIZING PROJECTS

Use the forms provided to plan your month's project. Each week, prioritize your project tasks and schedule them on the Project Priorities page at the front of this calendar.

PROJECT ANALYSIS: GARAGE, ATTIC AND/OR BASEMENT ORGANIZATION

Problem: Your garage, attic and/or basement holds everything from heirlooms to hardware. It's nearly impossible to find anything "stored" there, and much of it is damaged, useless or hopelessly outdated.

Solution: Go through the area, get rid of everything no longer needed or used, and organize the rest.

Project Goal: To organize the garage, attic and/or basement.

Benefits: Quick and easy access to stored items; adding potential for more active living space (convert the attic into a loft office; clear out the garage so two cars can be parked in it instead of one).

Visualization: Visualize your garage, attic and/or basement perfectly organized.

Affirmation: The garage, attic and/or basement are areas that are neat and clean, and provide more than enough space for active and practical use whenever I need it.

Estimate of Time Needed: Depends on how many areas you must organize and how big they are. Allow at least one full day for each area (garage, attic or basement). Schedule extra time needed on a consecutive day since it's better to do a major project like this all at once. If you plan to organize all three areas, schedule the days on your calendar.

Deadline: June 30

TO DO

- Measure available wall space for possible installation of extra shelving.
- Taking the measurements with you, shop for shelving, hooks, banker's boxes, bins and other containers.
- Working on one area at a time, remove as much as possible.
- Sort items into categories.
- Eliminate items that are damaged, useless or unnecessary.
- Install shelving, hooks and other space-saving organizers.
- Put items back into the area, keeping like items grouped together and stored in clearly labeled containers.
- Take unwanted items that are in good condition to a charitable organization.

Delegate as many tasks as possible. For example, get others to help haul items out of the area, sweep and clean, and install new shelves or hooks.

NEEDS CHECKLIST

You may want to invest in some space-savers and organizers for your garage, attic or basement. Exactly what you need will be determined by how you want to use these areas and what you want to store. You may need:

Shelving to hold storage boxes, bins and containers that group items by category

Hooks on the wall to hold bikes, tools, chairs, garden tools and such

Drawer dividers. Turn an old dresser into a hardware center with items divided in drawers by category.

Banker's boxes to store required legal and accounting records, mementos and holiday decorations

Dish or cat litter pans to hold items such as paintbrushes and small sports equipment

Large industrial containers with lids to store sports equipment or hazardous items such as sharp tools or yard chemicals

Establish a budget before you make your purchases. Call around to check prices and make a shopping list. Buy what you need and can afford, and then put those tools to work for you to complete your project.

SOURCES

- Home supply and variety stores
- Hardware stores
- Closet and organization stores

For more detailed information on how to complete this project, you may want to refer to my book *How to Conquer Clutter*.

ELIMINATE: GARAGE, ATTIC AND/OR BASEMENT CLUTTER

- College essays and notes
- Baby clothes (your kids are grown)
- High school letter sweater (moth-eaten)
- Rock collection
- Dried-up paint
- Broken VCR
- Ping-Pong table with three legs
- Receipts going back 20 years
- Old stacks of magazines and newspapers
- Mangled holiday wrapping supplies
- Tools and equipment too rusty to use
- Stash of empty boxes and bags
- Boxes of your children's old macaroni art
- Sets of dishes you never use
- Outdated furniture that needs to be fixed
- Old planters and chipped flowerpots
- Broken toys and sports gear
- Outdated office supplies and equipment

MASTER PLAN— STEPS TO SUCCESS

Start with one area, and concentrate on that space first. If that space is too cluttered for you to work efficiently, remove as much as possible to another area, where you have more room to sort items. Common categories include:

  Hardware, tools and paint supplies
  Auto supplies
  Seasonal furnishings
  Sports and camping equipment
  Legal and financial paper archives
  Miscellaneous mementos
  Holiday decorations
  Yard supplies and equipment
  Cleaning supplies

Organize the categories of items into bins and containers for easy storage and retrieval. Label all sides of the container clearly so the contents can be determined at a glance.

Add shelving. This can be metal industrial shelving, single shelves installed on the wall where necessary or freestanding bookcases. Use the shelves to hold uniformly sized boxes (with files, papers, mementos and decorations), to keep floor space unobstructed. Only store large items, such as major pieces of yard equipment, directly on the floor.

REWARD YOURSELF

Once you've organized your garage, attic and/or basement, give yourself a reward. Take in a ball game or do nothing but relax for an entire weekend. You deserve it.

PROJECT ANALYSIS

PROBLEM OR NEED

Describe a problem you want to correct, or outline something you need or want.

_____

_____

_____

_____

_____

_____

SOLUTION AND PROJECT GOAL

Write the solution to your problem or describe what you must do to get what you need or want.

_____

_____

_____

_____

BENEFITS

List the benefits that will result if you complete your project and achieve your goal.

_____

_____

_____

_____

VISUALIZATION

Describe how you see yourself and your surroundings after you have achieved your Project Goal.

_____

_____

_____

_____

_____

AFFIRMATION

Write an affirmation for success. Review it regularly and remind yourself of the ongoing benefits of your successfully completed project.

_____

_____

_____

_____

_____

ESTIMATE TOTAL TIME NEEDED FOR PROJECT

Make certain your estimate is realistic and you are willing to set that time aside.

_____

DEADLINE FOR PROJECT COMPLETION

A goal is just a dream with a deadline. Set a sensible deadline for success.

_____

TO DO

PROJECT: _____ **DEADLINE:** _____

THINGS TO DO	DATE SCHEDULED

DELEGATE

PROJECT: _____ **DEADLINE:** _____

TODAY'S DATE	TASK	DELEGATED TO	DEADLINE	DONE

NEEDS CHECKLIST

PROJECT: _____ **DEADLINE:** _____

List sources for information, services or products you need to complete your project. Note item size, quantity, color or other details. Call beforehand to check availability and price.

NEEDS	SOURCE	PHONE NUMBER	PRICE

NOTES

MASTER PLAN—STEPS TO SUCCESS

PROJECT: _____ DEADLINE: _____

WHERE TO START

_____

_____

_____

_____

_____

Make a detailed list of all actions needed to complete your project. Prioritize and schedule each task on a weekly basis. (Use the Project Priorities form and your monthly calendar for planning.) When each task is completed, cross it off your list.

ACTIONS TO TAKE	DATE SCHEDULED

ACTIONS TO TAKE	DATE SCHEDULED

"Desire is the key to motivation, but it's the determination and commitment to an unrelenting pursuit of your goals . . . that will enable you to attain the success you seek."

—Mario Andretti

PROJECT PLANNING

Use July's project planning forms to plan and/or complete a project of your choice. Mark key deadlines on your calendar.

IF YOU WANT TO GET ORGANIZED:

The urge to do nothing or to curl up with a good book in summertime can be very tempting. Instead of fighting the temptation to relax, July is a good time to *catch up on your reading*.

JULY PROJECT PRIORITIES

Week One _____

_____

_____

_____

Week Two _____

_____

_____

_____

Week Three _____

_____

_____

_____

Week Four _____

_____

_____

_____

Week Five _____

_____

_____

_____

JULY CALENDAR

SUNDAY	MONDAY	TUESDAY	WEDNESDAY

THURSDAY	FRIDAY	SATURDAY

SCHEDULING CHECKLIST

✔ Schedule appointments and standing obligations.

✔ Note special days such as birthdays and anniversaries.

✔ Schedule time for regular exercise.

✔ Make a date to give time and attention to someone special.

✔ Schedule a few hours each week of quiet time for yourself.

PRIORITIZING PROJECTS

Use the forms provided to plan your month's project. Each week, prioritize your project tasks and schedule them on the Project Priorities page at the front of this calendar.

PROJECT ANALYSIS: READING CATCH-UP

Problem: Stacks of magazines, journals or newspapers litter your home and office, and you've no idea when you'll get around to reading them all. Curling up with a good novel has become a total fantasy.

Solution: Go through all of the stacks of backed-up reading material, get rid of what's unnecessary, and catch up on the rest.

Project Goal: To catch up with your reading.

Benefits: By eliminating unnecessary reading materials, you'll have more time for what you really need—and want—to read.

Visualization: Visualize yourself with all of your reading caught up.

Affirmation: I read newspapers and trade journals in a timely fashion and put information I glean from them to immediate use. I have time each month to read books and magazines purely for enjoyment and relaxation.

Estimate of Time Needed: Depends on how much material you have to go through and how much reading you must (or want) to do. Allow at least one full day to go through your stacks, and another day to catch up on the reading itself. If it takes you more than two uninterrupted days, schedule the steps you need to take on your calendar.

Deadline: July 31

TO DO

- Gather all reading material in one area
- Eliminate as many publications as possible
- Clip articles
- Sort publications and articles into priority stacks
- Devote time to reading

Delegate as many tasks as possible. For example, have someone clip articles for you and presort magazines and trade journals by date (so you can discard outdated publications more quickly).

NEEDS CHECKLIST

To help you organize and whittle down your "must read" material, you may benefit from the following tools:

Scissors, stapler and staple remover for clipping articles

Bins, boxes or baskets to sort reading materials by category or priority order. Make one large bin your incoming *To Read* holder.

Magazine holders for magazines you keep for reference. Use the holders to categorize and store the magazines on a shelf.

SOURCES

- Office supply and stationery stores
- Office supply catalogs
- Office supply discount megastores
- Variety stores

For more information on how to complete this project, you can refer to my book *You Can Find More Time for Yourself Every Day*.

ELIMINATE: UNNECESSARY READING MATERIALS

- Outdated items such as old catalogs, price lists or publications that have been replaced by newer versions
- Any publications you do not really have

to or want to read

- Anything full of information you'll probably never use
- Journals automatically routed to you for no particular reason
- Publications more than three months old
- At least half of your overabundance of newspapers

MASTER PLAN— STEPS TO SUCCESS

Gather all of the publications and books into one large stack. If you have more than one stack, put the materials in boxes.

Look at each publication, eliminating as many as you can by recycling or throwing them out. Check the table of contents in the publications you're convinced you must read. If only one article is of interest, clip the article, staple it together, and recycle or throw away the rest of the publication.

Prioritize your *To Read* stack by sorting the articles and publications into categories. For example, you may want to sort into these categories:

- Professional
- General interest
- Reference and resource reading

Decide which publications and articles require your immediate attention, and which can be read later for relaxation. Devote at least a day to uninterrupted reading, beginning with the reading that is most important to you.

REWARD YOURSELF

Once you've caught up on reading, reward yourself. Be a couch potato for a day (without guilt). Or spend a day at the pool with the family. Give yourself a whole day of relaxation reading—read a mystery or science fiction novel in one sitting, and revel in the luxury of it!

PROJECT ANALYSIS

PROBLEM OR NEED

Describe a problem you want to correct, or outline something you need or want.

_____

_____

_____

_____

_____

_____

SOLUTION AND PROJECT GOAL

Write the solution to your problem or describe what you must do to get what you need or want.

_____

_____

_____

_____

BENEFITS

List the benefits that will result if you complete your project and achieve your goal.

_____

_____

_____

_____

VISUALIZATION

Describe how you see yourself and your surroundings after you have achieved your Project Goal.

_____

_____

_____

_____

_____

AFFIRMATION

Write an affirmation for success. Review it regularly and remind yourself of the ongoing benefits of your successfully completed project.

_____

_____

_____

_____

_____

ESTIMATE TOTAL TIME NEEDED FOR PROJECT

Make certain your estimate is realistic and you are willing to set that time aside.

_____

DEADLINE FOR PROJECT COMPLETION

A goal is just a dream with a deadline. Set a sensible deadline for success.

_____

TO DO

PROJECT: _____ DEADLINE: _____

THINGS TO DO	DATE SCHEDULED

DELEGATE

PROJECT: _____ **DEADLINE:** _____

TODAY'S DATE	TASK	DELEGATED TO	DEADLINE	DONE

NEEDS CHECKLIST

PROJECT: _____ **DEADLINE:** _____

List sources for information, services or products you need to complete your project. Note item size, quantity, color or other details. Call beforehand to check availability and price.

NEEDS	SOURCE	PHONE NUMBER	PRICE

NOTES

MASTER PLAN—STEPS TO SUCCESS

PROJECT: _____ DEADLINE: _____

WHERE TO START

_____

_____

_____

_____

Make a detailed list of all actions needed to complete your project. Prioritize and schedule each task on a weekly basis. (Use the Project Priorities form and your monthly calendar for planning.) When each task is completed, cross it off your list.

ACTIONS TO TAKE	DATE SCHEDULED

ACTIONS TO TAKE	DATE SCHEDULED

"There would be more leisure time if it weren't for the leisure time activities that use it up."

—Peg Bracken

PROJECT PLANNING

For many people, the heat of August is the perfect time to put projects and work aside and take a vacation. Use this month's forms to complete a project of your choice or to tackle one of the 11 organizing projects outlined in this planner. Or let August be the one month you forget all about projects and simply *relax and enjoy yourself!*

AUGUST PROJECT PRIORITIES

Week One _____

_____

_____

_____

Week Two _____

_____

_____

_____

Week Three _____

_____

_____

_____

Week Four _____

_____

_____

_____

Week Five _____

_____

_____

_____

AUGUST CALENDAR

SUNDAY	MONDAY	TUESDAY	WEDNESDAY

THURSDAY	FRIDAY	SATURDAY

SCHEDULING CHECKLIST

✔ Schedule appointments and standing obligations.

✔ Note special days such as birthdays and anniversaries.

✔ Schedule time for regular exercise.

✔ Make a date to give time and attention to someone special.

✔ Schedule a few hours each week of quiet time for yourself.

PRIORITIZING PROJECTS

Use the forms provided to plan your month's project. Each week, prioritize your project tasks and schedule them on the Project Priorities page at the front of this calendar.

PROJECT ANALYSIS

PROBLEM OR NEED

Describe a problem you want to correct, or outline something you need or want.

_____

_____

_____

_____

_____

_____

SOLUTION AND PROJECT GOAL

Write the solution to your problem or describe what you must do to get what you need or want.

_____

_____

_____

_____

BENEFITS

List the benefits that will result if you complete your project and achieve your goal.

_____

_____

_____

_____

VISUALIZATION

Describe how you see yourself and your surroundings after you have achieved your Project Goal.

_____

_____

_____

_____

_____

AFFIRMATION

Write an affirmation for success. Review it regularly and remind yourself of the ongoing benefits of your successfully completed project.

_____

_____

_____

_____

_____

ESTIMATE TOTAL TIME NEEDED FOR PROJECT

Make certain your estimate is realistic and you are willing to set that time aside.

_____

DEADLINE FOR PROJECT COMPLETION

A goal is just a dream with a deadline. Set a sensible deadline for success.

_____

TO DO

PROJECT: _____ DEADLINE: _____

THINGS TO DO	DATE SCHEDULED

DELEGATE

PROJECT: _____ DEADLINE: _____

TODAY'S DATE	TASK	DELEGATED TO	DEADLINE	DONE

NEEDS CHECKLIST

PROJECT: _____ **DEADLINE:** _____

List sources for information, services or products you need to complete your project. Note item size, quantity, color or other details. Call beforehand to check availability and price.

NEEDS	SOURCE	PHONE NUMBER	PRICE

NOTES

MASTER PLAN—STEPS TO SUCCESS

PROJECT: _____ DEADLINE: _____

WHERE TO START

_____

_____

_____

_____

_____

Make a detailed list of all actions needed to complete your project. Prioritize and schedule each task on a weekly basis. (Use the Project Priorities form and your monthly calendar for planning.) When each task is completed, cross it off your list.

ACTIONS TO TAKE	DATE SCHEDULED

ACTIONS TO TAKE | DATE SCHEDULED

"Successful people form the habit of doing what unsuccessful people don't like to do."

—Earl Nightingale

PROJECT PLANNING

Use September's project planning forms to plan and/or complete a project of your choice. Mark key deadlines on your calendar.

IF YOU WANT TO GET ORGANIZED:

If you have children, September is the perfect time to *organize the children's rooms.*

SEPTEMBER PROJECT PRIORITIES

Week One _____

_____

_____

_____

Week Two _____

_____

_____

_____

Week Three _____

_____

_____

_____

Week Four _____

_____

_____

_____

Week Five _____

_____

_____

_____

SEPTEMBER CALENDAR

SUNDAY	MONDAY	TUESDAY	WEDNESDAY

THURSDAY	FRIDAY	SATURDAY

SCHEDULING CHECKLIST

✔ Schedule appointments and standing obligations.

✔ Note special days such as birthdays and anniversaries.

✔ Schedule time for regular exercise.

✔ Make a date to give time and attention to someone special.

✔ Schedule a few hours each week of quiet time for yourself.

PRIORITIZING PROJECTS

Use the forms provided to plan your month's project. Each week, prioritize your project tasks and schedule them on the Project Priorities page at the front of this calendar.

PROJECT ANALYSIS: ORGANIZE CHILDREN'S ROOMS

Problem: The kids' closets and drawers are stuffed with outgrown clothes; toys, games and school supplies are strewn everywhere.

Solution: Go through everything and weed out what's no longer worn, enjoyed or useful. Organize the clothes, toys and school supplies that the kids need and use.

Project Goal: To organize the children's rooms.

Benefits: Kids can dress quickly and properly in clothes that fit. Homework will be streamlined with school supplies organized and easy to find. You won't be overwhelmed by the clutter and chaos created by dozens of toys and games that no one plays with. And the room will be easier to clean.

Visualization: Visualize all of your children's rooms perfectly organized.

Affirmation: My children's rooms are organized. The clothing in their closets and dressers fits, and is neatly folded or hung. School supplies are organized and easy to find, and there's a place for their toys, arts-and-crafts supplies and sports gear. Everything is age-appropriate, easy to find and put away.

Estimate of Time Needed: Depends on how many rooms you need to organize and how cluttered they are. Allow at least one full day. If it takes you longer, schedule the steps you need to do on your calendar.

Deadline: September 30

TO DO

- Measure the inside of closets, drawers and wall space.
- Taking the measurements with you, shop for organizing and space-saving containers and extra shelving and bookcases.
- Working on one room at a time, start with the closet and dresser, taking everything out and sorting it into categories.
- Eliminate items that are outgrown or never worn.
- Install closet space-savers, drawer dividers or extra shelving.
- Put items back into the closet and dressers, keeping like items together.
- Categorize and organize school supplies into desk drawers, bins or shelves.
- Categorize and organize arts-and-crafts supplies onto shelves in labeled containers, eliminating anything that's never used, dried up or damaged.
- Categorize and organize toys onto shelves and in labeled containers, eliminating those that are never used, broken beyond repair or no longer age-appropriate.
- Categorize and organize sports gear onto shelves and in labeled containers, eliminating equipment that's never used or broken beyond repair.
- Take unwanted items that are in good condition to a charitable organization.

Delegate as many tasks as possible. For example, let the children help weed out broken and useless items by presorting toys and crafts supplies into "good" and "bad" piles.

NEEDS CHECKLIST

Exactly which organizing tools and shelving you'll need will be determined by your children's ages and needs, as well as by how much space each child has for his or her belongings. You may need:

Shelving or bookcases to hold everything from sweaters to games to books. Store small items in containers and bins on the shelves.

Plastic hangers with a wire swivel hook to make it easier to hang clothing (wire or plastic hangers aren't flexible)

Labeled dishpans and kitty litter pans to separate categories of items—from socks to rock collections

Labeled plastic bins to separate and store anything that will fit—from doll clothes to 100 small rubber army men. Trash-can-like bins are perfect for grouping long, hard-to-store items, such as bats, hockey sticks and fishing poles. They are also handy for containing balls of all sizes.

Establish a budget before you make your purchases. Call around to check prices and make a shopping list. Buy what you need and can afford, and then put those tools to work for you to complete your project.

SOURCES

- Home supply and variety stores
- Hardware stores
- Closet and organization stores

For more detailed information on how to complete this project, you may want to refer to my book *How To Conquer Clutter*.

ELIMINATE: CLUTTER IN CHILDREN'S ROOMS

- Broken toys
- Toys that are not age-appropriate
- Outgrown clothing
- Gloves, mittens or socks with a permanently missing mate
- Dried-up arts-and-crafts supplies
- Stickers that don't stick
- Books that are not age-appropriate
- Ratty underwear
- Parts and pieces of things that can't be identified
- Games with permanently missing important pieces
- Old mimeographed school papers
- Outdated sports and school schedules
- Moldy macaroni art projects
- Outgrown Halloween costumes
- Old collections that have been cast aside

MASTER PLAN— STEPS TO SUCCESS

If you have several rooms to organize, begin with one and work on it until it's finished. Start by organizing the closet in the room.

Take everything out of the closet and the dresser. Group items into categories such as:

Shirts and blouses

Pants

Skirts

Dresses

Sweaters

Shorts

T-shirts

Sports clothing

Shoes
Underwear
Socks
Pajamas
Robes
Jackets and coats
Dressy outfits
Hats
Scarves and gloves

Refold items that belong on shelves and in drawers, and rehang clothes on plastic hangers with swivel hooks. Put items away in order, by category, and within easy reach of the child. Use drawer dividers to keep items organized inside dresser drawers. For example, shoeboxes in a drawer make it easier for kids to put items away neatly.

School Supplies. Gather and group in separate categories such as:

Pens and pencils
Paper
Notebooks and folders
Reference books
Scissors and miscellaneous supplies

Set up a study corner and store school supplies in that area. Use square bins or baskets to hold excess materials, and store the bins on shelves or bookcases in the room. Consider setting up an inexpensive two-drawer filing cabinet or rolling file cart to hold a selection of completed schoolwork. Store school art projects in the bottom of the rolling file cart or under the bed in a storage box.

Arts-and-Crafts Supplies. Gather and group in separate categories such as:

Markers, crayons and colored pencils
Drawing and other craft paper
Scissors and glue
Paints
Paintbrushes
Stickers

Toys. Gather and group in separate categories such as:

Dolls and doll accessories
Costumes and dress-up clothes
Action figures
Special collections
Board games
Books and magazines
Cars and trucks

Sports Gear. Gather and group in separate categories such as:

Balls
Ice and roller skates
Racquets
Flippers and goggles
Bats and hockey sticks
Helmets
Protective gear
Fishing poles and accessories

Containers and Shelves. Put the categories of arts-and-crafts supplies, toys and sports gear into containers placed on shelves. (See the Needs Checklist for types of containers to help keep items organized.) Clearly label all containers and bins so it's easy for the child to keep everything in its proper place.

Dresser drawers can be tough for kids to keep neat, so, as an alternative, use shelves that a child can reach rather than drawers wherever possible. For example, a small bookcase placed along a wall inside a closet can hold clothing such as:

T-shirts
Shoes and boots

Socks (in bin on shelf next to shoes)
Sweaters
Hats and gloves (in bin on shelf)
Sports clothing

Shelves can also hold arts-and-crafts supplies, books, toys, school supplies and some sports gear. Put the items directly on the shelves or in labeled bins on the shelves. Install shelves directly on the wall or place small bookcases strategically in the room. Out-of-season or rarely used items can be stored on harder-to-reach shelves—such as those over the closet rod in the closet.

REWARD YOURSELF

Once you've completed your project of organizing your children's rooms, give yourself a reward. Do something adultlike—get a sitter and treat yourself to an afternoon matinee, followed by dinner out. Or spend some fun time with the kids. The newly organized crafts in their room will make it easier and a lot more fun to do!

PROJECT ANALYSIS

PROBLEM OR NEED

Describe a problem you want to correct, or outline something you need or want.

_____

_____

_____

_____

_____

_____

SOLUTION AND PROJECT GOAL

Write the solution to your problem or describe what you must do to get what you need or want.

_____

_____

_____

_____

BENEFITS

List the benefits that will result if you complete your project and achieve your goal.

_____

_____

_____

_____

VISUALIZATION

Describe how you see yourself and your surroundings after you have achieved your Project Goal.

_____

_____

_____

_____

_____

AFFIRMATION

Write an affirmation for success. Review it regularly and remind yourself of the ongoing benefits of your successfully completed project.

_____

_____

_____

_____

_____

ESTIMATE TOTAL TIME NEEDED FOR PROJECT

Make certain your estimate is realistic and you are willing to set that time aside.

_____

DEADLINE FOR PROJECT COMPLETION

A goal is just a dream with a deadline. Set a sensible deadline for success.

_____

TO DO

PROJECT: _____ **DEADLINE:** _____

THINGS TO DO	DATE SCHEDULED

DELEGATE

PROJECT: _____ **DEADLINE:** _____

TODAY'S DATE	TASK	DELEGATED TO	DEADLINE	DONE

NEEDS CHECKLIST

PROJECT: _____ **DEADLINE:** _____

List sources for information, services or products you need to complete your project. Note item size, quantity, color or other details. Call beforehand to check availability and price.

NEEDS	SOURCE	PHONE NUMBER	PRICE

NOTES

MASTER PLAN—STEPS TO SUCCESS

PROJECT: _____ DEADLINE: _____

WHERE TO START

_____

_____

_____

_____

Make a detailed list of all actions needed to complete your project. Prioritize and schedule each task on a weekly basis. (Use the Project Priorities form and your monthly calendar for planning.) When each task is completed, cross it off your list.

ACTIONS TO TAKE	DATE SCHEDULED

ACTIONS TO TAKE | DATE SCHEDULED

"Nothing in this world can take the place of persistence. . . . The slogan 'press on' has solved and always will solve the problems of the human race."

—Calvin Coolidge

PROJECT PLANNING

Use October's project planning forms to plan and/or complete a project of your choice. Mark key deadlines on your calendar.

IF YOU WANT TO GET ORGANIZED:

"National Get Organized Week," falls in October, so this could be the time to get organized once and for all. Select any of the major organization projects in this planner, or use this month to conquer the small pockets of clutter in your life such as your briefcase, purse, car, desk pencil drawer and kitchen junk drawer. Whether your organization project is big or small, October is a good month to *organize and conquer pockets of clutter.*

OCTOBER PROJECT PRIORITIES

Week One _____

_____

_____

_____

Week Two _____

_____

_____

_____

Week Three _____

_____

_____

_____

Week Four _____

_____

_____

_____

Week Five _____

_____

_____

_____

OCTOBER CALENDAR

SUNDAY	MONDAY	TUESDAY	WEDNESDAY

THURSDAY	FRIDAY	SATURDAY

SCHEDULING CHECKLIST

✔ Schedule appointments and standing obligations.

✔ Note special days such as birthdays and anniversaries.

✔ Schedule time for regular exercise.

✔ Make a date to give time and attention to someone special.

✔ Schedule a few hours each week of quiet time for yourself.

PRIORITIZING PROJECTS

Use the forms provided to plan your month's project. Each week, prioritize your project tasks and schedule them on the Project Priorities page at the front of this calendar.

PROJECT ANALYSIS: ORGANIZING POCKETS OF CLUTTER

Problem: Your briefcase is choked with important papers and papers that should be filed or trashed. Your car looks like a rolling litter wagon. The pencil drawer in your desk is full of useless items, and the kitchen junk drawer is stuffed. Every time you must deal with one of these clutter-choked items or areas, you waste time finding what you need.

Solution: Identify the small pockets of clutter that get in your way regularly and organize those areas.

Project Goal: To organize small pockets of clutter in your life.

Benefits: Eliminate the daily frustrations that go with all the small pockets of clutter in your life. You'll be able to find the keys in your purse immediately; your briefcase will be a functional tool. Your pencil drawer will provide useful supplies when you need them, and the kitchen junk drawer will once again hold things you need and can find.

Visualization: Visualize small pockets of clutter of your life perfectly organized.

Affirmation: With even the smallest areas of my life organized, I am under less daily stress. I don't have to look for items buried in clutter, so my days are more productive, and I have more time for what I want to do.

Estimate of Time Needed: Depends on how many pockets of clutter you need to clean out and organize. Allow at least one uninterrupted day to tackle the clutter. If it takes you more than one full day, schedule the steps you need to do on your calendar.

Deadline: October 31

TO DO

- Measure the inside of any area (such as junk and pencil drawers) that could use organizers, dividers or space-savers.
- Taking the measurements with you, shop for the items you'll need.
- Work on one area at a time; take everything out and sort into categories.
- Eliminate items that are no longer useful.
- Install any helpful organizers or dividers.
- Put everything back, grouped into categories.

Delegate as many tasks as possible. Let someone else sort items like pens that do or don't work (a child can do this). If there's any cleaning to do, delegate that as well.

NEEDS CHECKLIST

The organizers and space-savers you'll need depend on what areas have become small pockets of clutter for you. You may need:

Drawer dividers for use in any drawer

File folders to label and use in your briefcase to keep papers logically sorted

Dishpans and kitty litter pans for grouping things like cleaning supplies and such

Tape racks to organize and store tapes

Turntables for inside cabinets to hold items (such as spices)

Purse organizers for organizing credit cards and checkbook. Cosmetic bags can hold cosmetics in your purse or briefcase.

Containers to hold everything from shoe polish to sewing supplies

Establish a budget before you make your purchases. Call around to check prices and make a shopping list. Buy what you need and can afford, and then put those tools to work for you to complete your project.

SOURCES

- Home supply and variety stores
- Department stores
- Closet and bath or organization stores
- Office supply and stationery stores
- Catalogs for home or office supplies
- Hardware stores

For more information, you may want to refer to my book *How to Conquer Clutter*.

ELIMINATE: MISCELLANEOUS CLUTTER

- Spices that you never use, are hard as a rock or have bugs
- Medicines that have expired
- Anything that is too dried out to use
- Pens that don't write
- Business cards of people you don't remember and don't need to know
- Scraps of paper with meaningless writing on them
- Socks with serious holes
- VCR and audio tapes that you don't like and never play
- Exotic utensils that you never use
- Expired coupons or coupons for food you don't eat
- Receipts that are not tax-deductible or of any other use
- Expired schedules and invitations
- Hardware that goes to items you no longer own
- Items that are broken and not worth repairing
- Pieces of crockery that you've been meaning to glue together "someday"

MASTER PLAN— STEPS TO SUCCESS

Make a list of all the small pockets of clutter you want to tackle. These can include:

Purse and briefcase

Car

Sock drawer

Utensil and junk drawer in kitchen

VCR or audio tapes

Shoe polish supplies

Medicine cabinet and makeup drawer

Desk pencil drawer

Cleaning supplies

Spice cabinet in kitchen

Hardware: screws, nails, etc.

Sewing supplies

Manicure supplies

Begin with one area and work on that until you're finished. Then move to the next.

Regardless of which small pocket of clutter you organize, the procedure is the same. Simply use the Five Super Steps to Getting Organized from page 2 of this planner. Tackling one area at a time, apply the steps until you are finished. Then move on to the next area and repeat the process.

REWARD YOURSELF

Once you've conquered the small pockets of clutter in your life, give yourself a reward. Sit around and watch the leaves fall, get a manicure, or get in a quick game of miniature golf. By organizing those small pockets of clutter in your life, you have relieved yourself of countless daily frustrations.

PROJECT ANALYSIS

PROBLEM OR NEED

Describe a problem you want to correct, or outline something you need or want.

_____

_____

_____

_____

_____

_____

SOLUTION AND PROJECT GOAL

Write the solution to your problem or describe what you must do to get what you need or want.

_____

_____

_____

_____

BENEFITS

List the benefits that will result if you complete your project and achieve your goal.

_____

_____

_____

_____

VISUALIZATION

Describe how you see yourself and your surroundings after you have achieved your Project Goal.

_____

_____

_____

_____

_____

AFFIRMATION

Write an affirmation for success. Review it regularly and remind yourself of the ongoing benefits of your successfully completed project.

_____

_____

_____

_____

_____

ESTIMATE TOTAL TIME NEEDED FOR PROJECT

Make certain your estimate is realistic and you are willing to set that time aside.

_____

DEADLINE FOR PROJECT COMPLETION

A goal is just a dream with a deadline. Set a sensible deadline for success.

_____

TO DO

PROJECT: _____ DEADLINE: _____

THINGS TO DO	DATE SCHEDULED

DELEGATE

PROJECT: _____ **DEADLINE:** _____

TODAY'S DATE	TASK	DELEGATED TO	DEADLINE	DONE

NEEDS CHECKLIST

PROJECT: _____ **DEADLINE:** _____

List sources for information, services or products you need to complete your project. Note item size, quantity, color or other details. Call beforehand to check availability and price.

NEEDS	SOURCE	PHONE NUMBER	PRICE

NOTES

_____

_____

_____

_____

_____

_____

_____

_____

_____

_____

_____

_____

_____

_____

_____

_____

MASTER PLAN—STEPS TO SUCCESS

PROJECT: _____ DEADLINE: _____

WHERE TO START

_____

_____

_____

_____

_____

Make a detailed list of all actions needed to complete your project. Prioritize and schedule each task on a weekly basis. (Use the Project Priorities form and your monthly calendar for planning.) When each task is completed, cross it off your list.

ACTIONS TO TAKE	DATE SCHEDULED

ACTIONS TO TAKE	DATE SCHEDULED

"As one goes through life one learns that if you don't paddle your own canoe, you don't move."

—Katharine Hepburn

PROJECT PLANNING

Use November's project planning forms to plan and/or complete a project of your choice. Mark key deadlines on your calendar.

IF YOU WANT TO GET ORGANIZED:

With the holidays just ahead, use this month to schedule and plan for the season so you're left with fond memories rather than exasperated feelings of exhaustion. November is a good time to *get organized for the holidays*.

NOVEMBER PROJECT PRIORITIES

Week One _____

_____

_____

_____

Week Two _____

_____

_____

_____

Week Three _____

_____

_____

_____

Week Four _____

_____

_____

_____

Week Five _____

_____

_____

_____

NOVEMBER CALENDAR

SUNDAY	MONDAY	TUESDAY	WEDNESDAY

THURSDAY	FRIDAY	SATURDAY

SCHEDULING CHECKLIST

✔ Schedule appointments and standing obligations.

✔ Note special days such as birthdays and anniversaries.

✔ Schedule time for regular exercise.

✔ Make a date to give time and attention to someone special.

✔ Schedule a few hours each week of quiet time for yourself.

PRIORITIZING PROJECTS

Use the forms provided to plan your month's project. Each week, prioritize your project tasks and schedule them on the Project Priorities page at the front of this calendar.

PROJECT ANALYSIS: PREPARING FOR THE HOLIDAYS

Problem: The holiday season customarily finds you overcommitted, underfunded and completely exhausted from trying to get everything done on time.

Solution: Start early in November, and make a plan for all aspects of the holidays, from sending cards and buying gifts to entertaining and holiday travel.

Project Goal: To get organized for the holidays.

Benefits: Enjoy the holidays rather than be exhausted by them.

Visualization: Visualize yourself having a wonderful time this holiday season.

Affirmation: I always plan for the holiday season, and I start early so I can avoid last-minute scrambles to get things done. I spend my time having fun with friends and family. I'm not afraid to delegate some tasks; I consider it money well spent to hire services to help me. Because of my planning and time-saving techniques, I enjoy the holiday season immensely.

Estimate of Time Needed: Depends on how you plan to spend your holidays. You may want to cut back on the material aspects of the holidays and focus more on spending time with loved ones. Or you may decide to get away from it all and take a trip. If you stick with all the traditions of sending cards, hosting big dinners, buying gifts for everyone and attending parties, you should allow at least a week to 10 days in November to get everything done. If you don't finish, you can schedule more time later. (Shopping is discussed in detail in December.)

Deadline: Set your own deadline according to when the holiday(s) fall. Remember that the earlier you start, the earlier you finish, giving you more time to enjoy the actual holiday.

TO DO

The specifics of your To Do list depends entirely on how much or how little you want to do for the holidays. If ever there was a time to delegate, this is it. It's the quickest route to doing less but enjoying the holidays more. Some ways to delegate:

- Hire a cleaning service for right before and right after your party or dinner. Hire a teenager to help clean or polish the silver. Or hire a professional organizer to help you conquer major household clutter before company comes.
- Hire a caterer, or make your event a potluck affair. Get baked goods at the bakery. Get a precooked ham, or buy a turkey already dressed.
- Hire a teenager to get out the holiday decorations, unpack everything and sweep up.
- Use a personal shopper or errand service. Call department store personal shopping services. Order by catalog and let them mail out-of-town gifts. (More shopping tips are in December.)
- Get stamps by mail and hire a senior citizen or teenager to address your cards. Or put your list on a computer (use a computer secretarial service).
- Use a travel agent for all travel arrangements.

- Break big projects into smaller tasks, and let each family member take on two or three tasks at a time.
- Trade tasks with friends and relatives. If you hate to shop but love to cook, ask a friend who loves to shop (but hates to cook) to do your shopping (give him or her a list and money), and you can cook some special dishes for the friend to freeze and serve.

NEEDS CHECKLIST

Make a detailed list depending on your particular holiday needs. What you need will probably fall under these three categories:

Gifts

Groceries

Services

Establish a budget before you make your purchases and sign up services. Check prices and make a detailed shopping list, and decide what services you'll use. Buy (and hire) what you need and can afford, and then put those tools and services to work for you to ensure that you are organized and can spend your time enjoying the season rather than working yourself to a frazzle.

SOURCES

Sources can include stores and services of all kinds.

- Department stores
- Gift and specialty shops
- Grocery and gourmet shops
- Liquor stores
- Catalogs
- Cleaning services
- Shopping and errand services
- Caterers and party planning services
- Teenagers and senior citizens
- Secretarial services
- Travel agents

For more detailed information on how to find the time for this project, you may want to refer to my book *You Can Find More Time for Yourself Every Day*.

ELIMINATE: HOLIDAY HASSLES

- Hosting elaborate dinners that are all work and no fun
- Sending greeting cards if the tradition has become meaningless for you
- Going to parties when you'd rather be home with your feet up
- Traditions that require lots of work and are barely noticed (such as baking cookies when cookies from a bakery would be received just as well)
- Entertaining people you really don't like
- Traveling from one set of in-laws to another in a single day just to keep everyone happy. One solution to this problem is to alternate holidays, spending one at each in-law's, with the third rotation at your house (they can come to you).
- Buying more than you have to (see December for more on this)

MASTER PLAN— STEPS TO SUCCESS

Evaluate how you have spent your holidays in the past and make a commitment to how you want to spend this holiday season. For example, if you want to spend less money, or you want more tradition in your observance, or you want to get away from it all this year, decide that now. Once you have made a firm commitment about exactly how you want to spend and remember your holidays, you can make plans to do just that.

List everything you must do to make this holiday season one that will be memorable without being exhausting. Whatever you do, resist the urge to overcommit yourself. You don't have to say yes to every party invitation or request for holiday help that comes your way. Nor do you have to spend all of your free time shopping and cooking for others. Make sure your list covers what and who is really important to you; then nurture that list, and politely decline everything else.

Cleaning. List all the special cleaning tasks that must be done, such as cleaning the silver and clearing out the guest room closet. Clean five pieces of silverware each night when you do the dinner dishes. In three weeks, you'll have cleaned 75 pieces of silver.

Entertaining. This year, reconsider what and how you host. Rather than spending days getting ready for a major dinner at your house, consider hosting a brunch, open house, or a dessert and coffee get-together. These types of events are very nice and are less expensive and time-consuming than an all-out dinner. If you must do a major meal at your house, start a potluck tradition. When guests offer to bring something, let them! Or ask them to bring their favorite holiday dish. And when guests come into the kitchen to help with the cleanup, don't turn them down. The cleanup will get done in half the time, and the kitchen can be the best place in the house to congregate for good conversation while that work is being done.

Decorating. Note how much, if any, decorating you will do this year, and when the decorations need to be up. Decorate the house one room at a time, and do the yard and exterior in two days instead of one.

Shopping. Decide who you want to buy gifts for; then decide exactly what you'll buy for each person. (Time-saving shopping techniques and gift ideas are discussed in more detail in December.) If you want to get a head start on your shopping in November, buy three gifts per week in November; by the end of the month you'll already have a dozen gifts. Or, you might want to start some new traditions. If buying gifts is creating a time and financial burden for you, don't give in to the pressure to purchase so many gifts. Tell others of your pared down gift list, and ask them not to buy for you either. Tell yourself that children don't need dozens of gifts, when several will do. Ask extended family members to draw names, and do the same at the office. You'll save all kinds of financial worry and shopping time, and chances are others will be relieved to be able to cross you off their list as well.

Cards and Invitations. If you plan to send greeting cards, update your list of names and addresses. Address five cards each evening; by Thanksgiving, you'll have more than 100 cards ready to mail. If you're sending party invitations for New Year's Eve, address 10 invitations every Monday night before bed. In six weeks, you'll have at least 60 invitations ready to mail.

Travel. If you'll be traveling, decide where and when you want to go. If you'll be driving some distance, join an auto club and get route and hotel information for your trip. The following week, plan your exact route and make any necessary reservations.

Look at each category and determine the deadlines for getting everything done. Start well in advance of each deadline so you don't wind up in a last-minute frenzy.

REWARD YOURSELF

Since the holidays start in November and don't conclude until New Year's Day, your project of getting organized for the holidays probably will continue into December. But if you started early in November and did something significant each week to get a good head start, give yourself a reward. When you're shopping, buy something for yourself. If you're in the grocery store picking up items for a dinner you're hosting, get something special for you alone to enjoy one night before bed. Or get away from it all for a weekend so you can recharge for the holidays that fall in December and early January.

PROJECT ANALYSIS

PROBLEM OR NEED

Describe a problem you want to correct, or outline something you need or want.

_____

_____

_____

_____

_____

_____

SOLUTION AND PROJECT GOAL

Write the solution to your problem or describe what you must do to get what you need or want.

_____

_____

_____

_____

BENEFITS

List the benefits that will result if you complete your project and achieve your goal.

_____

_____

_____

_____

VISUALIZATION

Describe how you see yourself and your surroundings after you have achieved your Project Goal.

_____

_____

_____

_____

_____

AFFIRMATION

Write an affirmation for success. Review it regularly and remind yourself of the ongoing benefits of your successfully completed project.

_____

_____

_____

_____

_____

ESTIMATE TOTAL TIME NEEDED FOR PROJECT

Make certain your estimate is realistic and you are willing to set that time aside.

_____

DEADLINE FOR PROJECT COMPLETION

A goal is just a dream with a deadline. Set a sensible deadline for success.

_____

TO DO

PROJECT: _____ **DEADLINE:** _____

THINGS TO DO	DATE SCHEDULED

DELEGATE

PROJECT: _____ DEADLINE: _____

TODAY'S DATE	TASK	DELEGATED TO	DEADLINE	DONE

NEEDS CHECKLIST

PROJECT: _____ **DEADLINE:** _____

List sources for information, services or products you need to complete your project. Note item size, quantity, color or other details. Call beforehand to check availability and price.

NEEDS	SOURCE	PHONE NUMBER	PRICE

NOTES

MASTER PLAN—STEPS TO SUCCESS

PROJECT: _____ DEADLINE: _____

WHERE TO START

_____

_____

_____

_____

_____

Make a detailed list of all actions needed to complete your project. Prioritize and schedule each task on a weekly basis. (Use the Project Priorities form and your monthly calendar for planning.) When each task is completed, cross it off your list.

ACTIONS TO TAKE	DATE SCHEDULED

ACTIONS TO TAKE	DATE SCHEDULED

"We write our own destiny. We become what we do."

—Madame Chiang Kai-Shek

PROJECT PLANNING

Use December's project planning forms to plan and/or complete a project of your choice. Mark key deadlines on your calendar.

IF YOU WANT TO GET ORGANIZED:

Even if you started organizing for the holidays in November, the likelihood is that you will have more shopping to do. (If you haven't even begun to get organized for the holidays, see November for more on how to plan and organize your holidays.) The first few weeks of December are your last chance to complete any shopping you must do. Obviously, December is the time to *organize and complete all holiday shopping.*

DECEMBER PROJECT PRIORITIES

Week One _____

_____

_____

_____

Week Two _____

_____

_____

_____

Week Three _____

_____

_____

_____

Week Four _____

_____

_____

_____

Week Five _____

_____

_____

_____

DECEMBER CALENDAR

SUNDAY	MONDAY	TUESDAY	WEDNESDAY

THURSDAY	FRIDAY	SATURDAY

SCHEDULING CHECKLIST

✔ Schedule appoint-
ments and standing
obligations.

✔ Note special days
such as birthdays and
anniversaries.

✔ Schedule time for
regular exercise.

✔ Make a date to give
time and attention to
someone special.

✔ Schedule a few
hours each week of
quiet time for your-
self.

PRIORITIZING PROJECTS

Use the forms pro-
vided to plan your
month's project. Each
week, prioritize your
project tasks and
schedule them on the
Project Priorities page
at the front of this cal-
endar.

PROJECT ANALYSIS: HOLIDAY SHOPPING

Problem: You never have time to shop, so you end up racing around at the last minute, battling chaos and crowds. The giving spirit turns into "I give in," with you buying items that aren't on your list and are over your budget. By the time the gift is wrapped and presented, you're so worn out you wish that gift-giving holidays could be abolished.

Solution: Plan *before* you go shopping. Start early, use time-saving techniques (see page 179), and shop according to your plan and budget.

Project Goal: To organize and complete all of your holiday shopping.

Benefits: Give yourself an early deadline to complete your shopping, and stick to your shopping plan and budget, so that you'll be able to enjoy rather than dread the art and act of giving.

Visualization: Visualize yourself with all of your shopping and gift wrapping done well in advance of the holidays.

Affirmation: I am organized and ready for the holidays in advance. My shopping is done in the true spirit of gift-giving rather than in the spirit of obligation. My budget is intact, and I have time to spend with friends and family in a relaxed and joyful way.

Estimate of Time Needed: Depends on how much shopping you must do. This might be the year to cut your list back. How much time you save or spend on shopping is entirely up to you. Allow at least one full day, and start early in the month so you can schedule more days later (but still well in advance of the holiday).

Deadline: Set your own deadline according to when the holiday falls. Remember that the earlier you start, the earlier you finish, giving you more time to actually enjoy the holiday.

TO DO

- Make a list of people to buy gifts for.
- Trim the list as much as possible.
- Decide what to buy each person and note it on the list.
- Order as much as you can by phone.
- Call stores to check availability and price on items before you go shopping.

Delegate as much of your shopping and wrapping as possible. For example, order via catalogs and buy gifts like tickets by phone. (Other delegating ideas can be found in November's Master Plan on page 163.)

NEEDS CHECKLIST

Make a detailed list of the gifts you plan to buy. Your purchases will probably fall under these categories:

Toys

Clothes

Tapes, CDs and books

Gift certificates and tickets to events

Sports-related items

Food and beverage gifts

Other

Establish a budget before you purchase your gifts. Check prices and make a detailed shopping list, organized by category. Buy what you need and can afford, and don't let the commercialism of the season derail your shopping plan and budget.

SOURCES

Sources can include stores and services.

- Department stores
- Gift and specialty shops
- Liquor stores and gourmet shops
- Catalogs and ticket outlets
- Shopping and errand services
- Professional services that provide gift certificates

For more detailed information on how to find time for this project, you may want to refer to my book *You Can Find More Time for Yourself Every Day*.

ELIMINATE: SHOPPING HEADACHES

- Buying gifts you can't afford and worrying about how much money you spend on each gift (it's the thought that counts)
- Buying a gift just because someone buys you one
- Overbuying for the children
- Buying gifts for relatives you barely know
- Wasting time wrapping and mailing gifts out of town (let the store or catalog company do it)
- Impulse buying

MASTER PLAN— STEPS TO SUCCESS

List all the people you want to give a gift to. Remove as many names from the list as possible so you can give gifts to people who matter the most to you. (Call people and ask them to remove your name from their list as well. They'll probably be relieved.)

Decide—in advance—what to purchase for each person on your list, making sure that the item is within your budget.

Often the most appreciated gift can be purchased without a lot of effort. You can save time and still buy great gifts by using some of these ideas:

Catalogs. Order from catalogs and let them wrap and mail the gift.

Gift Certificates from a department, specialty, record or bookstore, or from a professional service (such as a massage or a day at the beauty salon or spa).

Tickets to concerts, plays and other events can be ordered by phone, and make great gifts.

Money is often the best gift of all. Children, teenagers and newlyweds, in particular, like gifts of money.

Wine or Gourmet Food. Pick up several bottles of wine or gourmet food items and keep them on hand for last-minute gifts or to take with you when you go to a party.

Organize Your List and Make Calls. Organize your gift list and order as much as you can by phone. Before you go out to shop, call the stores to check the price and make certain they have what you're looking for.

Consolidate Shopping Trips. Plan your shopping trips locally, buying as much as possible in one area. When you're finished there, go to the next area.

REWARD YOURSELF

If you started early and completed your shopping well in advance of the gift-giving day, the pleasure you get out of the holiday season will be your reward.

PROJECT ANALYSIS

PROBLEM OR NEED
Describe a problem you want to correct, or outline something you need or want.

_____

_____

_____

_____

_____

_____

SOLUTION AND PROJECT GOAL
Write the solution to your problem or describe what you must do to get what you need or want.

_____

_____

_____

_____

BENEFITS
List the benefits that will result if you complete your project and achieve your goal.

_____

_____

_____

_____

VISUALIZATION

Describe how you see yourself and your surroundings after you have achieved your Project Goal.

_____

_____

_____

_____

_____

AFFIRMATION

Write an affirmation for success. Review it regularly and remind yourself of the ongoing benefits of your successfully completed project.

_____

_____

_____

_____

_____

ESTIMATE TOTAL TIME NEEDED FOR PROJECT

Make certain your estimate is realistic and you are willing to set that time aside.

_____

DEADLINE FOR PROJECT COMPLETION

A goal is just a dream with a deadline. Set a sensible deadline for success.

_____

TO DO

PROJECT: _____ **DEADLINE:** _____

THINGS TO DO	DATE SCHEDULED

DELEGATE

PROJECT: _____ **DEADLINE:** _____

TODAY'S DATE	TASK	DELEGATED TO	DEADLINE	DONE

NEEDS CHECKLIST

PROJECT: _____ **DEADLINE:** _____

List sources for information, services or products you need to complete your project. Note item size, quantity, color or other details. Call beforehand to check availability and price.

NEEDS	SOURCE	PHONE NUMBER	PRICE

NOTES

MASTER PLAN—STEPS TO SUCCESS

PROJECT: _____ DEADLINE: _____

WHERE TO START

_____

_____

_____

_____

_____

Make a detailed list of all actions needed to complete your project. Prioritize and schedule each task on a weekly basis. (Use the Project Priorities form and your monthly calendar for planning.) When each task is completed, cross it off your list.

ACTIONS TO TAKE	DATE SCHEDULED

ACTIONS TO TAKE	DATE SCHEDULED

About the Author

Stephanie Culp is also the author of *You Can Find More Time for Yourself Every Day*, *Streamlining Your Life*, *How to Get Organized When You Don't Have the Time*, *How to Conquer Clutter*, and *Conquering the Paper Pile-Up*. She owns the productivity consulting firm, The Organization. She also is a national speaker and trainer specializing in topics that help people and businesses get organized, save time, and manage paper more effectively. For more information on her services contact:

Stephanie Culp
The Organization
P.O. Box 108
Oconomowoc, WI 53066

(414) 567-9035
Fax (414) 567-0736